JOHN L███████N

C000051985

Copyright © 1997 Johnny Rogan
This edition © Copyright 1997 Omnibus Press
(A Division of Book Sales Limited)

Edited by Chris Charlesworth
Cover & Book designed by 4i
Picture research by Nikki Russell

ISBN 0.7119.5599.9 Order No.OP47831

All rights reserved. No part of this book may be reproduced in any form or by any electronic or
mechanical means, including information storage or retrieval systems, without permission in writing
from the publisher, except by a reviewer who may quote brief passages.

Exclusive Distributors:
Book Sales Limited, 8/9 Frith Street, London W1V 5TZ, UK.
Music Sales Corporation, 257 Park Avenue South, New York, NY 10010, USA.
Music Sales Pty Limited, 120 Rothschild Avenue, Rosebery, NSW 2018, Australia.

To the Music Trade only:
Music Sales Limited, 8/9 Frith Street, London W1V 5TZ, UK.

Photo credits: Front cover: Don McCullin/Magnum; back cover: Penny Tweedie/Retna;
all other pictures supplied by Richard Dilello, Harry Goodwin, LFI, Barry Plummer, Retna & Rex Features.
Every effort has been made to trace the copyright holders of the photographs in this book but one or two were unreachable.
We would be grateful if the photographers concerned would contact us.

Printed in the United Kingdom by Ebenezer Baylis & Son, Worcester.

A catalogue record for this book is available from the British Library.

The right of Johnny Rogan to be identified as the author of this work has been asserted by him in accordance
with the Copyright, Designs and Patents Act 1988.

OMNIBUS PRESS
LONDON · NEW YORK · SYDNEY

CONTENTS

INTRODUCTION & ACKNOWLEDGEMENTS

The Beatles' recording career has been documented extensively in countless books, including a companion volume in this series. Such is not the case with John Lennon's solo work, however, which receives relatively short shrift in biographies and is generally regarded as insufficiently substantial to warrant a full-scale study in its own right. This guide attempts to rescue Lennon's work from the proprietorial clutches of Beatles' mythology. Beginning with his first collaboration with Yoko Ono, it continues through his solo years, carefully analysing each of his albums. It is striking to consider that the space of time between John Lennon's death and the publication of this book is virtually the same as that from the Beatles' first Parlophone recording in 1962, through the whole of his solo career up until his murder in 1980. Time is indeed a jet plane, as Bob Dylan once suggested.

Despite the obvious importance of Lennon's solo work, it is regrettable to report that no serious attempt has been made at remastering the entire catalogue for the CD generation. It is to be hoped that this will be rectified in the near future.

Listening to Lennon's complete works was both a challenge and a joy, made more comfortable and reassuring by a handful of works that dare to see him as more than Beatle John. I would like to thank fellow Omnibus author John Robertson whose *The Art And Music Of John Lennon* and *Lennon* were extremely valuable as both reference works and silent sounding boards for discussion and argument.

John Lennon was probably the best interviewee in the history of rock and his incisive comments on music and life are captured in such books as Jann Wenner's *Lennon Remembers*, David Sheff's *The Playboy Interviews,* and *The Lennon Tapes*, a transcript of the BBC interview conducted by Andy Peebles. All these were invaluable sources.

Other books that proved enlightening were Jon Wiener's brilliant *Come Together: John Lennon In His Time*,

Anthony Fawcett's *One Day At A Time* , *The Lennon Companion* (edited by Elizabeth Thomson & David Gutman) and *The Rolling Stone* Editors' *The Ballad Of John And Yoko*.

Greatest thanks is reserved for Peter Doggett, who was an ever patient recipient of calls concerning the most important and obscure areas of Lennon's recording career. His knowledge and appreciation were greatly valued and encouraged me to write a larger and more penetrating guide than originally anticipated by the publishers of this series.

For contributing some rare memorabilia: thanks to John Tobler and Adrien Van Clute.

Finally, hellos to John Regan, who first played me 'John Lennon/Plastic Ono Band' in 1970; to Alan Russell, who championed Lennon's name in the Buckingham Gate years; and, recalling Lennon's last days, to Gill Chester for being, quite possibly, the most inspiring person I ever met in my entire life.

JOHNNY ROGAN

Two Virgins.

"When two great Saints meet it is a humbling experience. The long battles to prove he was a Saint."—Paul McCartney

Unfinished Music No. 1. Two Virgins. Yoko Ono/John Lennon.

UNFINISHED MUSIC NO. 1: TWO VIRGINS

RELEASED: NOVEMBER 1968

[ORIGINAL UK ISSUE: APPLE (S)APCOR 2]

John Lennon had already been experimenting with home taping long before Yoko Ono came into his life, but there is no doubt that she was the catalyst in pushing him towards avant-garde experimentation. They had first met in November 1966 at John Dunbar's Indica Gallery, a full 18 months before this album was recorded. Lennon was heavily into LSD at the time and in the wake of The Beatles' groundbreaking 'Revolver' he seemed intent on immersing himself in every mind-expanding experience that the counter culture had to offer. Yoko Ono's Unfinished Paintings And Objects exhibition at the Indica appealed to Lennon's sense of the absurd with its overpriced artefacts such as the Sky Machine labelled $1,500 that "produces nothing when a coin is deposited". Later, Lennon vividly recalled the strong impression left by the show and that strange first encounter with Yoko Ono: "I got word that this amazing woman was putting on a show, and there was something about people in bags, and it was going to be a bit of a happening. So I went down to a preview of the show. There was an apple on sale there for £200. I thought it was fantastic. I got the humour in her work immediately. There was another piece which really decided me for or against the artist – a ladder which led to a painting which was hung on the ceiling. I climbed the ladder, looked through a spy glass and in tiny letters it said, 'Yes'. I felt relieved. John Dunbar insisted she say hello to the millionaire. She came up and handed me a card which said, 'Breathe' on it, so I just went [pants]. This was our first meeting!"

When he browsed through the exhibition catalogue, Lennon learned that there was more to Ono's art than expensive whimsy. Her writing betrayed a philosophic air, which would have appealed to the Beatle who had written such songs as 'The Word' and 'Tomorrow Never Knows'. Two weeks before recording

'Strawberry Fields Forever' (with its key line "Nothing Is Real"), Lennon had been looking at the following prose in her catalogue: "Man is born, educates himself, builds a house and a life and then all that vanishes when he dies. *What is real? Is anything real?* A thing becomes real to us when it is functional and necessary to us. As long as we strive for truth we live in self-induced misery, expecting in life something that is not an illusion. If we recognise that nothing is true or illusory... then we can proceed from there on to be optimistic and swallow life as it comes."

As John and Yoko were both married, their contact over the next year was sporadic. She sent him a copy of her book *Grapefruit*, which he found both fascinating and infuriating, depending on his mood and patience level. Before long, he was bombarded with postcards bearing cryptic messages such as "Watch all the lights until dawn", "Go to the horizon – measure it" and "Boil water and watch until it evaporates". Although she had already infiltrated his mind and would soon invade his household, he still insisted to his wife Cynthia:

"She's just another nutter wanting money for all that avant-garde bullshit."

As Lennon's marriage frosted over, so his interest in "avant-garde bullshit" increased. While Cynthia was persuaded to holiday abroad, John made the bold decision to invite Yoko to his Weybridge house. On the evening of May 20, 1968, they consummated their artistic, musical and sexual union with this abstract collage of electronic sounds. "I was always shy with Yoko," John insisted, when recalling that evening for the readers of *Playboy* magazine. "My ex-wife was away somewhere and Yoko and I did acid. We had never made love. Because I was shy, instead of making love, we went upstairs and made tapes. I had this room full of different tapes and loops where I wrote Beatles stuff. So we made a tape all night. She was doing her funny voices and I was pushing all different buttons on my tape recorder and getting sound effects. Then, as the sun rose, we made love. That was it. That was 'Two Virgins'. "

The *audio-vérité* album consisted of 30 minutes of voices, distorted instruments and various sound effects, including bird calls, falling buildings and snatches of music hall songs. The famous Yoko wail opened the work, with Lennon providing growling feedback on his guitar and screaming back at her. At one point, John says, "Who's there?" as Yoko's ghoulish whine segues into a tolling bell. There are also elements of humour, with Lennon adopting a Wilfred Pickles persona and announcing, "It's just me, Hilda, I'm home for tea". On Side 2, Yoko's wailing becomes more eerie and intense and there is a momentary element of melodrama as Lennon urges, "Go on then". Towards the end, John appears to imitate a sung Mass for a few seconds, but the idea is undeveloped. "I've had enough now, thank you," he announces wearily, "let's get this over with, if you don't mind", at which point the record concludes. For most contemporaneous listeners, the album must have sounded like a discordant indulgence, while its low volume recording virtually invited surface noise after a handful of plays. For the Lennons, of course, it was a stimulating

voyage of discovery. Overall, the intention of the work, as underlined in its title, was to create a soundscape that suggested a return to lost innocence.

The Edenic concept still gripped Lennon's imagination when he was considering the album's artwork. With Adam and Eve in mind, he decided upon a provocative sleeve whose notoriety would far outlast any comments on the album's aesthetic or musical appeal. "Originally, I was going to record Yoko, and I thought the best picture of her for an album would be her naked," he reasoned. "I was just going to record her as an artist. We were only on those kind of terms then. So, after that, when we got together, it just seemed natural for us, if we made an album together, for both of us to be naked. Of course, I've never seen me prick on an album or photo before... The album also says: 'Look, lay off, will you? It's two people – what have we done?' "

Yoko Ono said that the nude shot was John's idea. "I suppose he just thought it would be effective," she pointed out. "He took the picture himself with an automatic camera. It's nice. The picture isn't lewd or anything... We'd be the first to be embarrassed if anyone were to invite us to a nude party."

Such protestations of modesty left many of her detractors unconvinced. The sleeve was generally regarded at the time as either exhibitionist, smutty or pornographic. The participants' insistence that they were "very shy people" was greeted with equal scorn. Perhaps the best summation of this media derision can be seen in the footage of their later bed-in at Montreal, where cartoonist Al Capp sarcastically waves a cover of the album in the air and announces: "If that isn't a picture of two shy people, I'd like to know what shyness is... I think everybody owes it to the world to prove that they have pubic hair. And you've done it. I applaud you for it... and I tell you that's one of the greatest contributions to enlightenment and culture of our time."

Lennon had wanted to release 'Two Virgins' at the earliest opportunity but his choice of artwork resulted in a six-month delay, while his record company considered the implications. In order to avoid prosecution, it was decided that the album should be placed in a brown paper bag, a fate that had previously been considered for 'Sgt. Pepper's' when Brian Epstein panicked over possible litigation from its illustrious cover stars. While the controversy over the proposed sleeve continued, Lennon feigned innocent incredulity about the fuss he and Yoko were causing. "We had known each other two years by then," he insisted. "So... the record and the album cover of us naked was a way to show purity. Everybody was sort of upset. The fact that two people were naked. We thought it was insane that everybody was so upset about it."

One major obstacle they faced was the urbane chairman of EMI, Sir Joseph Lockwood. Not surprisingly, he was concerned about the impact that the album might have on the career of The Beatles, not to mention the reputation of his record company. What would the shareholders think? As John Lennon pointed

out: "'Two Virgins' was a big fight. It was held up... Sir Joseph Lockwood was a nice, nice guy... He said he understood it and he'd do everything he could to help us. Then, when we tried to put it out, he sent a personal note to everybody saying, 'Don't print it. Don't put it out'. So we couldn't get the cover printed anywhere."

Lennon's ironic comments on Lockwood's "nice guy" image were unfair on one level. In the moral climate of 1968, full frontal nudity on an album cover was bound to cause offence, particularly in Britain. What should have irked Lennon even more was the appalling attitude that the EMI chairman betrayed towards Yoko Ono. His prejudices were regrettably consistent with the prevailing public and media view of the time. When later recalling his first meeting with Ono, he said: "I wasn't sure if *it* was a human being or an animal". At a second meeting he insulted her with the quip: "Why don't you show Paul [McCartney] naked. He's so much better looking than you."

McCartney may not have been entirely convinced by the merits of 'Two

Virgins' but he did his best to win over Lockwood and was supportive enough to contribute an extravagantly portentous and grammatically confusing sleeve note, which read: "When two great Saints meet it is a humbling experience. The battles to prove he was a saint."

Sainthood, real or imagined, was never likely to persuade EMI or Capitol to distribute the offending disc, irrespective of the protective brown paper bag, whose outside featured a pointed description of Adam and Eve's nudity taken from the Book of Genesis. "EMI killed our album 'Two Virgins' because they didn't like it," Lennon added with cold disdain.

As the first release on Apple, 'Two Virgins' gained lots of publicity, but few sales. In the UK, it was distributed by Track, the label run by The Who's managers Kit Lambert and Chris Stamp. On the original pressing there were no banding or track listings, just two sides of 'Unfinished Music'. Stateside distribution was handled by the small independent Tetragrammaton, which suffered a setback when 30,000 copies of the disc were impounded in New Jersey for breaching parochial obscenity laws.

Lennon later came to regard the display of nudity as a political act, albeit one unappreciated by the proletariat. "Working class people reacted against our openness about sex," he said. "They are frightened of nudity, they're repressed in that way, as well as others."

When the album finally appeared in November 1968, it reached the shops a mere week before The Beatles' celebrated double album. That same month, Yoko had a miscarriage and John pleaded guilty to a trumped-up charge of marijuana possession. It was the unhappiest of times and 'Two Virgins' already seemed *passé* to its creators who were about to complete another experimental work. "It was a bum album," Yoko noted with mischievous irony. Nevertheless, it remains a defining moment in Lennon's creative life and a testament to his love of improvisation, mixed with humour and child-like wonder.

STEREO EAS-80701

UNFINISHED MUSIC NO. 2: LIFE WITH THE LIONS

RELEASED: MAY 1969

[ORIGINAL UK ISSUE: ZAPPLE 01]

While The Beatles' legend inexorably entered its final phase, the John and Yoko saga continued to excite world attention. In addition to the reams of newspaper print documenting their public appearances and personal upheavals, the duo provided these experimental albums of 'Unfinished Music', which almost functioned as aural diaries of their recent troubled history. During the month that this album was recorded, Yoko suffered a miscarriage and John protected her by pleading guilty to illegal possession of cannabis, for which he was fined £150, plus 20 guineas costs. That charge would have serious implications later in his career when US authorities threatened him with deportation. The sleeve of this album captures the sadness and drama of both the above incidents. On the front, Yoko is pictured in a hospital bed, clutching an apple, while John sits patiently on some cushions spread on the ward floor next to her. On the back cover, John and Yoko are pictured surrounded by police after "being dragged out of the police station". The scene receives a further commentary in the album subtitle *'Life With The Lions'*, a sardonic pun on the cosy British wartime radio show *Life With The Lyons*. There's a similar ironic tone in the manufacturing note: "Made in merrie England", plus a slight dig at the conservatism of The Beatles' producer in the words "'No Comment' – George Martin" placed above the album title.

Contemporaneous critics and public alike perceived these records as akin to the ravings of a madman and a madwoman. Few appreciated that Yoko Ono had solid avant-garde credentials stretching back to the Fifties, when she had studied music and art at the prestigious Sarah Lawrence College, before dropping out to stage events at her loft in Greenwich Village. After marrying her second husband Tony Cox, Yoko staged many talked-about exhibitions, provocative films and various writings, which spread her fame in art circles around the world. What she brought to John Lennon was a knowledge of conceptual and performance art, heavily influenced by such key figures as John Cage, Andy Warhol, La Monte Young and that New York group of painters, poets and musicians collectively named Fluxus.

Unsurprisingly, perhaps, Lennon felt that avant-garde was a limiting adjective to apply to the work of his beloved. "Well, that's the only word you can use for it," he regretted. "But, I think a label like avant-garde defeats itself. You learn to have avant-garde exhibitions. The fact that avant-garde can have an exhibition defeats the purpose of avant-garde because it's already formalised and ritualised, so it's not avant-garde. But that was the only word... that was the word that was applied to her and her ilk."

The improvisational records that John and Yoko produced during this period still sound eccentric, although they clearly borrowed from current avant-garde thinking. John Cage's belief in encouraging audience participation as part of the artistic event had already been demonstrated by Yoko in her exhibitions. It is here too in these experimental records. Even the subtitle of the first two Lennon/Ono works suggested a work of art in flux. In explaining the idea behind the concept 'Unfinished Music', Yoko told critic John Cott: "If you listen to it, maybe you can add to it or change it or edit or add something in your mind. The unfinished part that's not in the record – what's in you, not what's in the record, is what's important. The record is just there to stimulate what's in you, to make it come out."

For listeners accustomed to pop and rock, these albums were seen as inexplicable and indulgent. Today, the world has caught up with the ideas, if not the aesthetic appreciation. As *New York Times'* critic John Rockwell rightly observes: "It is difficult to explain or excuse vanguard art to those who don't know it or can't stand it. To them, it can seem like deliberate provocation, with its apparently tedious length, deafening volume, aggressive behaviour towards an innocent audience and other unpleasantries."

It is ironic to consider that most of the people who bought these albums were likely to be disgruntled Beatles collectors whose acquisitive mentality demanded that they owned every recorded utterance by the Fab Four. For passing punters interested in esoterica, the purchasing motive was more likely intellectual curiosity or novelty hunting rather than genuine enthusiasm. Of course, The Beatles saw it differently. For them, avant-garde was another important new experiment, like folk rock, ragas, sound collages and all the other trends that they had helped popularise during the second half of the Sixties. The newly created Zapple label, which issued this record and George Harrison's experimental 'Electronic Sounds' on the same day, was intended as an outlet for all sorts of improvisational and spoken word recordings. Instead, the label ceased operation after its first two releases – an apposite enough comment on the public's reaction to these arcane releases. Limited availability and a relatively small number of pressings have ensured that both volumes of 'Unfinished Music' remain collectors' items, but those that are still in circulation are likely to be near mint copies. Repeated listening was never high on the list of priorities for serious or casual purchasers and, given the topicality of the material coupled with notions of instant disposability, it is doubtful whether John and Yoko ever expected anyone to play these records too long after their release date.

In our current age where everything, no matter how obscure or seemingly uncommercial, appears to warrant a re-release on CD, these works are still vinyl rarities and look likely to remain so into the next century.

CAMBRIDGE 1969

Two months before the release of 'Life With The Lions', John and Yoko performed before an audience of approximately 500 people at Lady Mitchell Hall, Cambridge, on March 2, 1969. "I was invited to Cambridge to do a number, a sort of avant-garde number," Yoko explained. "And they didn't realise we were together... They didn't realise then and they invited me, and so I said, 'All right what shall I do?' And John was saying, 'Well, it's all right, why don't you go?' And they were saying: 'Well are you going to bring a band?' So John said, 'Well, I'm the band, but don't tell them. I'll be the band'."

For Lennon the opportunity to appear on-stage with Yoko was irresistible. This was his first public performance since the glory days of The Beatles and the results could hardly have been more contrasting. Instead of adoring fans, he was faced with an avant-garde audience which regarded him suspiciously as an interloper from the unsavoury commercial world of rock music. It was salutary for John to empathise with the feelings of Yoko, who had suffered far worse criticism when daring to attend Beatles sessions.

The concert, which took up an entire side of this album, begins with Yoko quietly announcing: "This is a piece called 'Cambridge 1969'." Her familiar screaming

vocal dominates the recording, while Lennon provides accompanying feedback through his lead guitar. As the performance progresses, Ono's screams undulate, then gradually become more intense. It's tough listening for non-avant gardists, but there is a noticeable sense of calm in those more palatable moments when the feedback is lowered. Towards the end, the pair are joined by jazz avant-garde players John Stevens and John Tchakai. A cymbal is then used to vary the sound pattern before the listener is once more enveloped by the swirling feedback. It is just possible to hear Yoko intoning the words 'Free Hanratty', which emerge as whispers through the speakers. Just as the track reaches its conclusion a saxophone is introduced and the mood changes subtly once more. It leaves the listener wishing that the jazz musicians had joined the pair earlier in the piece to break up or vary the unrelenting scream/feedback routine... but that was no doubt the point of the exercise.

Lennon's recollection of the evening was suitably deadpan. "It was supposed to be an avant-garde jazz thing," he noted vaguely. "And there was this guy John Tchakai who was apparently a famous avant-garde sax guy, or jazz sax guy – I don't know any of them. A few people that I don't remember the names of – they were there too. And I turned up as her band and the people were looking and saying: 'Is it? Is it?' I just had a guitar and an amp and that was the first time I'd played that style, just pure feedback and whatever is on that track. The audience was very weird because they were all these sort of intellectual, artsy-fartsies from Cambridge and they were uptight because the rock 'n' roll guy was there, even though I wasn't doing any rhythm. If you hear it, it's pure sound because what else can you do when a woman's howling? You just go along with it."

NO BED FOR BEATLE JOHN

This track, previously available on a flexi-disc in the March 1969 edition of the art magazine *Aspen*, documents the sad third week of November 1968, when Yoko had her miscarriage at London's Queen Charlotte Hospital. John had vowed to stay by her bedside throughout her stay, but a shortage of beds meant that he had to sleep on the floor, propped up by cushions. This track was akin to an elegy for "John Ono Lennon II", the miscarried foetus whose remains were placed in a coffin and buried in a secret location.

The mood of the piece is reflective and sombre and sung like a requiem mass. Yoko reads or rather chants lines from the newspapers of that week, telling us how John "lost his hospital bed yesterday to a patient". There is also an account of the furore surrounding the impending release of 'Two Virgins' that same month. While Yoko chants, John provides a counter harmony with his reading, which is tantalisingly out of earshot for most of the piece. Overall, this performance is by far the most interesting and inventive track on the album and it is rather surprising that Lennon did not choose to repeat the idea of word chanting on one of his mainstream solo recordings. One can only imagine what someone like Phil Spector would have conjured if presented with this concept by Lennon.

BABY'S HEARTBEAT

Towards the end of Yoko's troubled pregnancy, John taped a few seconds of the heartbeat of her unborn baby. Upon returning to the studio, he put this through a tape loop, creating a track in excess of five minutes. The result was this strange piece which sounds like a cross between a stereo test record and the soundtrack of an underwater adventure story. The baby's life force undulates eerily between the speakers, before suddenly stopping.

TWO MINUTES SILENCE

Borrowing the idea from John Cage's controversial concert piece *4' 33"*, John and Yoko offer us two minutes of silence. This fits perfectly in the context of this album as a haunting requiem for the dead baby. Drama and expectancy is added to the listening process through the use of such a long silence, which also offers the chance to meditate on the couple's loss or, indeed, anything else that comes into your mind.

RADIO PLAY

This track was also previously premièred as a give-away flexi-disc with the magazine *Aspen*. The punning title refers to the concept which consists of "playing with a radio". While a static screech is created by turning a radio on and off in rapid succession, John and Yoko's muted conversation can be heard in the background. Along the way, we hear John attempting to phone the Ambassador Hotel and trying to reach his aide Anthony Fawcett. The rhythm of the piece gradually changes as Lennon continues to fiddle with the radio set, making a more intense sound that resembles the screeching of a violin. There's a certain child-like wonder here in the way they attempt to create new and unexpected sounds from unusual sources. Inevitably, though, the track goes on for far too long, by which time curiosity is replaced by impatience. It's not a piece that easily invites repeated listening.

STEREO EAS-80702

WEDDING
ALBUM

WEDDING ALBUM

RELEASED: NOVEMBER 1969

[ORIGINAL UK ISSUE: SAPCOR 13]

The wedding of John and Yoko, two weeks after the nuptials of Paul McCartney and Linda Eastman, symbolised the final severing of a musical partnership that had once seemed inseparable. It would be several months more before the world realised that Lennon/McCartney was a dead brotherhood. In the meantime, John and Yoko continued to transform the circumstances of their daily lives into aural events. Not surprisingly, their marriage proved a living documentary that served as a romantic but salutary saga for the world. The pair had intended to marry on a cross-channel ferry to France, but they were denied access to the ferry *Dragon* at Southampton Docks due to passport irregularities. After consulting Beatles aide Peter Brown, they flew to the Rock of Gibraltar on March 20, where they were married in the British Consulate building. They were in and out of the country in an incredible 70 minutes. As Lennon explained: "We chose Gibraltar because it is quiet, British and friendly. We tried everywhere else first. I set out to get married on the car ferry and we would have arrived in France married. But they wouldn't do it. We were no more successful with cruise ships. We tried embassies. But three weeks' residence in Germany or two weeks' in France were required."

The events that followed the marriage were international news. After spending a couple of days at the Plaza Athenee Hotel in France, during which they met painter Salvadore Dali, they announced their intention to stage a "bed-in" for peace to take place in Amsterdam. One week later, the world's media descended on Room 902 of the Amsterdam Hilton Hotel, eager to document a salacious story. Instead, they found the Lennons sitting in bed, modestly clad in white pyjamas, while holding hands. Despite frequent derision from various media pundits, Lennon sold the story of peace in the same way that he related more prosaic Beatles activities: "We're staying in bed for a week to register our protest against all the suffering and violence in the world."

Throughout the week, the pair were at their most engagingly humorous and won over several cynical reporters who saw some perverse logic in their bed-in. Cartoonists loved the event and newspapers were full of depictions of "bed peace", usually featuring world leaders tucked up uneasily together. Newspaper pundits in search of new angles called in doctors and psychiatrists to analyse the implications. "Modern technique is to get even unfit people out of bed as soon as possible so that they can recover their strength," a medic suggested. "I should think they will feel very wonky when they get up." Psychiatrist Dr Ellis Stungo admitted he was baffled: "I can't get a firm line on their behaviour." Despite this, he was clearly willing to have a stab at explaining their hidden motivations: "It is sheer exhibitionism but one would have thought that

they had had so many opportunities to publicise themselves that their need would be satisfied by now. Perhaps it may be they feel their acclaim is waning, they need to feel acclaimed and this exhibition is a way of restoring security to them. On the other hand, it may be that they are both so unattractive and know that they are unpopular, so this is a way of trying to justify themselves – trying to show everyone that theirs is a tremendous romance of which they are not ashamed."

In addition to the countless commentaries from brow-creasing columnists on the rights and wrongs of the bed-in, there were numerous letters to the press from Joe Public. Some were scathing, some conciliatory and a few featured a tongue-in-cheek humour which would have appealed to Lennon. "The seven-day lie-in by John Lennon makes sense, not as a means of achieving world peace, but as a rest cure," one reader suggested. "This is the way to get away from the madding crowd unless it calls at your bedside. I am convinced that the health of the nation would improve if every husband and wife had three days in bed in turn – waited on hand and foot. The only time we get a three-day lie-in is when we go down with 'flu. The Government should cancel a Bank Holiday and introduce a Bed Holiday. Or why not a national lie-in?"

The selling of peace was also promoted through "bagism", another Yoko-influenced concept which required them to hide away in a white bag while conducting a press conference. Startled and sceptical interrogators at the Hotel Sacher in Vienna were reduced to asking such teasing questions as "How do we know it's you?"

There was further proof of Lennon's enduring commitment to Yoko soon after when, in a simultaneous fit of disenchantment with British imperialism, he elected to change his middle name from Winston to Ono. Although he would shortly deny faith in all belief systems, Lennon, at this point, still saw some significance in numerology, stressing: "Yoko changed her name for me. I've changed mine for her. One for both; both for each other. She has a ring; I have a ring. It gives us nine 'O's between

us, which is good luck. Ten would not be good luck."

While the newspapers continued to document the bed-ins and the Acorns For Peace campaign (in which world leaders were sent acorns to plant for peace), the Lennons were systematically filming their own lives. The Amsterdam Hilton bed-in had been regarded as a pivotal moment in their public lives – not just as a cry for peace but as a celebration of marriage. A *cinéma-vérité* film of the event was captured in documentary form on *Honeymoon*, while the audio equivalent was this commemorative 'Wedding Album'.

In addition to a two-sided record, this ornate box set featured various items of marital memorabilia, including a copy of their marriage certificate, a photo of a slice of wedding cake, four passport-sized photos taken in a booth, a poster featuring scenes from the wedding, a black and white postcard of the bed-in at the Amsterdam Hilton Hotel and a booklet of press cuttings detailing, in both amusing and gruesome reportage, the ridicule and condescension heaped upon them in the name of journalism. As John explained to the BBC: "It was our way of sharing our wedding with whoever wanted to share it with us. We didn't expect a hit record out of it. That's why we called it 'Wedding Album'. You know, people make a wedding album, show it to the relatives when they come round. Well, our relatives are the... what you call fans, or people that follow us outside. So that was our way of letting them join in on the wedding."

What John failed to mention was that the fans had already savoured the wedding story on record six months earlier, courtesy of The Beatles' chart-topping 'The Ballad Of John And Yoko', which humorously and poignantly detailed the tribulations of the pair at the hands of the authorities and the media. As Lennon had caustically observed: "the way things are going, they're going to crucify me". Intriguingly, the excellent single that documented John's union with Yoko was recorded by himself and Paul McCartney. At this point, John was still willing to use The Beatles' name to docu-

ment his and Yoko's trial by media, which meant that a well deserved number 1 record could be achieved in the UK, a statistic never to be accomplished by the later Plastic Ono Band. Using Paul as a creative foil to relate the ballad of John and Yoko was an irony that few noted, then or since. Clearly, though, John felt it was appropriate that he and Yoko should release their own avant-garde version of recent events for posterity. Needless to say, the resulting 'Wedding Album' was never likely to be a best seller but it remains a prized collectors' item. Although it was the last of their avant-garde albums trilogy, Lennon was determined that more should follow. "We're trying to do these things at the time they are happening," he pointed out. "We'd like to be able to produce them as fast as newspapers and television can. It will be a constant autobiography of our life together – and it will go on the rest of our lives."

JOHN AND YOKO

After changing his middle name from Winston to Ono, John celebrated his new bonding with Yoko by recording this experimental piece with her. Employing a microphone in the shape of a stethoscope, they taped several seconds of their respective heartbeats. John then consigned these to a mastertape, making a loop by which the sounds were repeated for 22 minutes. These were then played back while the Lennons added a mantra, intoning their names 'John And Yoko' for the duration of the recording. Drawing an analogy between Ono's film-making and this performance, the pseudonymous author John Robertson noted: "In the same way that the purity of Yoko's film *Bottoms* has been spoilt by the inclusion of semi-humorous voice-overs, so the beauty of the original statement – the two hearts pounding together to create a womb-like, mysterious pattern of sound – was subverted by the addition of the couple's voices. Having made the transition from 'Baby's Heartbeat' to their own, the experiment wasn't repeated."

Whether the two voices detract from the power of the two hearts beating is debatable. The track actually begins with the scrunching of an apple, after which the chants continue for an entire album side. John and Yoko manage to convey a variety of emotional responses while uttering their names, sometimes sounding petulant, loving, quizzical, frustrated and agonised. They whisper, shout, scream, purr, yearn and plead, while alternating the speed of their intonation to suggest everything from complete desolation to orgasmic joy. The major problem in appreciating the piece is not the combination of voice and sound, which works reasonably well, but the interminable length of the exercise which strains the listener's patience and attention span after the first few minutes have elapsed. At the end, they finish off the apple they had begun eating some 20 or more minutes before. It is tempting and probably quite correct to find symbolism in the Lennons devouring an Apple, given the state of the company at the time of the recording.

AMSTERDAM

The famous John and Yoko bed-in at the Amsterdam Hilton attracted journalists from all over the world and the Lennons decided to capture the event on record. For an entire 25-minute side of an album, the listener is allowed to eavesdrop on an *audio-vérité* best of the bed-in. It commences with John announcing "OK, Yoko", after which his spouse sings 'John John (Let's Hope For Peace)'. The performance is chanted in traditional Japanese style, with instrumentation and background effects which, overall, sound much more impressive than the later "rock" version performed by the Plastic Ono Band on 'Live Peace In Toronto'. Its major weakness is John's interjections, which sound as intrusive as some of Yoko's contributions to his rock songs. Developing the song, Yoko implores "Oh John, let's hope for peace for our children, for our countries, for our world, for our future..."

Yoko's performance is followed by an interview about the peace campaign, which manages to mix hippie left-wing rhetoric with fleeting examples of the Lennon humour. Recorded in London after the Amsterdam bed-in, it displays Lennon in confident mood, sounding articulate and persuasive. Yoko enters controversial territory, blaming the world, as much as Hitler, for the persecution of the Jews. They then discuss political history, with references to various acts of imperialism and peace attempts through the ages. Lennon eventually interrupts with the admission: "I'm as violent as the next man... we're violent people. I prefer myself non-violent. I prefer my friends when they're non-violent... I prefer to live in peace."

The scene then switches and after hearing seagulls and other sound effects we're taken back in time to Amsterdam, as John strums "Day In Bed". In this section, we eavesdrop on the Lennons waking up for their bed-in. "Good morning", John yawns, as journalists gather. He orders tea and brown toast from room service and is presented with a dog from a peace-loving visitor. He then reads some humorous extracts from the news-papers spread before him, as a sitar is played in the background. Photo shoots and interviews follow. One reporter attempts to return to the early Beatles' days and, failing to remember the correct title 'Love Me Do', asks John about their first record 'Do You Love Me'. "Not particularly," Lennon replies sardonically.

John next strums and sings "Goodbye Amsterdam" and Yoko replies with an impromptu song "Stay In Bed... Grow Your Hair", with an acoustic backing borrowed from the melody of The Beatles' 'Because'. As the side reaches its close, Lennon intones the traditional nursery rhyme, "Goodnight, sleep tight...", leaving Yoko to sum up the event. "What a beautiful day," she observes, "Very tiring though". A final bash at a new anthem follows as they chant "Grow Your Hair. Bed Peace. Hair Peace". The track ends with what sounds like an aeroplane revving up.

Overall, 'Amsterdam' works reasonably well as an aural extract from the bed-in and is suitably varied and entertaining in its contents to warrant more than a cursory listen.

LIVE PEACE IN TORONTO 1969

RELEASED: DECEMBER 1969

[ORIGINAL UK ISSUE: APPLE CORE 2001]

The live début of Lennon's Plastic Ono Band at the Toronto Rock 'n' Roll Revival Festival at the Varsity Stadium on September 13, 1969, proved one of the most spontaneous and unlikely happenings of the era. Co-promoter John Brower had phoned Apple Records at the last minute and invited John and Yoko to attend, no doubt in the hope of drumming up some publicity for the event.

His request seemed over-optimistic but there were good reasons for assuming that Lennon might look favourably upon the event. A few months before he had flown to Montreal for a celebrated bed-in at the Queen Elizabeth Hotel, during which a star-studded guest list had sung along to a new anthem, 'Give Peace A Chance'. Even the country's president Pierre Trudeau had spoken of Lennon with tolerance and respect. After receiving an invitation to plant acorns for peace the minister quipped: "I don't know about acorns, but I'd like to see him if he's around. He's a good poet."

Although it was unlikely that Lennon would return to Canada so soon, Brower's seemingly doomed festival included some interesting names. The mercurial Lennon was intrigued by the line-up of rock 'n' roll legends set to appear, a list that included Chuck Berry, Jerry Lee Lewis, Little Richard, Gene Vincent, Bo Diddley and Fats Domino. As Lennon's PR Anthony Fawcett recalled: "He had hardly said hello before he was agreeing to go – on the condition that he and his band could play live at the Revival."

The decision was a testament to Lennon's love of Fifties rock 'n' roll and his willingness to create instant happenings. Remarkably, he had not even conceived the band who would play their first gig the following night. With extraordinary rapidity, he pulled together a seemingly makeshift group comprising bassist Klaus Voormann (the Hamburg pal who had contributed the front sleeve of 'Revolver'), Apple session drummer Alan White, plus celebrated guitarist Eric Clapton and the ubiquitous Yoko Ono. The following day, Lennon slept in and threatened to pull out of the concert and send some flowers instead. Luckily, he changed his mind and joined the assembled crew on a later flight.

The trip to Toronto was memorable in more ways than one. Much to their astonishment, Lennon confided in the musicians that he was leaving The Beatles and offered them the chance to work with him on future projects. It was clear, however, that The Plastic Ono Band would be a fluid unit without a formal line-up. "The Plastic Ono Band is a conceptual band that never was," Lennon insisted. "There never had been any members of it... It wasn't like a Wings or whatever, where you had a name and you belong to it. There's nobody ever in that band, there are no members."

For "the band that never was", there remained the problem of selecting a suitable set list. Lennon had jotted down some rock 'n' roll evergreens that they could all perform, but their attempts at rehearsing on the plane proved desultory at best. Meanwhile, the Canadian media was blasting out news of Lennon's imminent arrival and starstruck kids were heading for Toronto in the hope of witnessing an historic event. By late afternoon, there were over 27,000 spectators in the stadium. On arrival, Lennon conducted a press conference, laced with fist-thrusting political rhetoric, proclaiming: "The power doesn't belong with Mr Trudeau, Mr Wilson or Mr Nixon. We are the power. The people are the power. And as soon as people are aware that they have the power, then they can do what they want. And if it's a case of they don't know what to do, let's advertise to them to tell them they have an option. They've all got a vote. Vote for peace, folks."

Backstage at the Varsity Stadium,

The Plastic Ono Band barely had time to continue their rehearsal before they were due on stage. Lennon was already vomiting at the prospect, as pre-performance nerves and heroin withdrawal took their toll. As the song annotations below explain though, the show was not the disaster it might have been but a modest success. "It was fantastic," Lennon recalled in a BBC interview. "It was just getting dark. The lights were just going down. This was the first time I ever heard about this, I'd never seen it anywhere else – they all lit candles, or lights, and the sun was going down. There was 50-60,000 people. All these candles lit up and it was really beautiful. The vibes were fantastic, and we did the string of rock 'n' roll stuff."

Lennon's determination to release the concert as a live album was met with resistance by his record label. "We tried to put it out on Capitol, and Capitol didn't want to put it out," he complained. "They said, 'This is garbage. We're not going to put it out with her screaming on one side and you doing this sort of live stuff'. And they just refused to put it out. But we finally persuaded them that people might buy this. Of course it went gold..."

The Toronto show was also filmed, but D.A. Pennebaker's movie of the event (provisionally titled *Sweet Toronto* and later renamed *Keep On Rockin'*) was not completed until the following year, by which time it was decided that The Plastic Ono Band's performance should not be included. It was another 19 years before the set finally appeared commercially on home video, complete with a number of additional Yoko Ono squeals that had been deleted from the album recording.

BLUE SUEDE SHOES

"Get your matches ready, The Plastic Ono Band..." announces compere Kim Fowley as Lennon and friends take the stage. "We're just going to do numbers we know because we've never played before," John explains, after which they begin tentatively with this Carl Perkins' classic. The metallic rasp of Clapton's lead guitar set against Lennon's confident vocal works well and the feel is reminiscent of the old BBC sessions during the early days of Beatlemania. "We just wrote this list," Lennon said of their impromptu set. "I hadn't even got the words to any of the songs... 'Blue Suede Shoes' and a couple I hadn't done since Liverpool in the Cavern and that's all we could do. We went on and we were so nervous because we didn't know what we were doing." The sense of spontaneity merely added to the unfolding drama.

MONEY

Memories of early Beatles' performances are reinforced as the band tackle the Berry Gordy song that so brilliantly closed 'With The Beatles'. Here, Lennon's vocal is unaccompanied and you miss McCartney's distinctive harmony and familiar reply line, "That's what I want". Although Lennon will soon be undertaking primal therapy, he studiously avoids the raucous screeching that characterised The Beatles' recording of this number, preferring a more restrained approach.

DIZZY MISS LIZZY

After finishing 'Money', Lennon recalls turning to Eric Clapton in a vain attempt to decide what to play next. The guitarist responded with a shrug of the shoulders but John recovered his memory sufficiently to kick-start another rock 'n' roll favourite. He had played this 1958 Larry Williams song many times during his youth, and it was previously the closing track on 'Help!' This version is understandably uncertain in places as the group gradually attempts to find its way into the performance. Despite some nervy moments, Lennon responds well to the challenge of playing without a proper rehearsal. "I can't remember when I had such a good time," he later enthused. "We did all the old things from the Cavern days in Liverpool. Yoko, who you can say was playing bag, was holding a piece of paper with the words to the songs in front of me. But then she suddenly disappeared into her bag in the middle of the performance and I had to make them up because it's so long since I sang them that I've forgotten most of them. It didn't seem to matter."

YER BLUES

Lennon sounds more expressive here as he resurrects one of the darker moments from The Beatles' 1968 double album. He had previously performed the song in a line-up with Eric Clapton, Keith Richard, Mitch Mitchell and Yoko on the unreleased Rolling Stones' film *Rock 'n' Roll Circus*. Clapton's familiarity with the composition ensures that this searing version is memorable, with 'Revolution' style guitar work to the fore.

COLD TURKEY

"We've never done this number before, so best of luck," announces Lennon, after which they tackle his harrowing account of heroin withdrawal. Taken at a slightly faster pace than the single version, the song features some jagged guitar work interspersed with effective vocal interjections from Yoko Ono. At one point Lennon had to berate the audience for not responding enthusiastically enough to his new composition, although this was edited out of the released recording. The

performance proves as uncompromising as the subject matter, which is hardly surprising in view of Lennon's physical state. "I just threw up for hours until I went on," he confessed. "Nearly threw up during 'Cold Turkey'. I could hardly sing any of them. I was full of shit."

GIVE PEACE A CHANCE

This spirited version of Lennon's peace anthem was particularly memorable for its humorous ad-libbing ("masturbation, castration, United Nations and Teddy Roosevelt"). At one point, he pays passing tribute to British comedian Tommy Cooper, a name presumably unfamiliar to his Canadian audience. The comedy was appropriate, given Lennon's view of himself and Yoko as the world's clowns. But beneath the elongated word play the song's sentiments were bitingly insistent. "I wanted to write something that would take over from 'We Shall Overcome'," Lennon explained. "I don't know why. Maybe because that was the one they always sang. I thought why doesn't somebody write one for the people now, the songs that they go and sing on the buses even, and not just love songs."

DON'T WORRY KYOKO (MUMMY'S ONLY LOOKING FOR HER HAND IN THE SNOW)

"And now Yoko's going to do her thing right over you," Lennon announces. An extraordinary version of this anthem to daughter Kyoko follows, complete with the references to "mummy's only looking for her hand in the snow" missing from the single recording issued as the B-side of 'Give Peace A Chance'. As the song reaches agonising pitches of intensity, Lennon and Clapton lock into an instrumental groove, which reinforces Yoko's intense vocal exhortations. They seem likely to develop the song into an elongated jam but, regrettably, it ends after 4 minutes 16 seconds.

JOHN JOHN (LET'S HOPE FOR PEACE)

The audience barely has time to recover before Yoko segues into this eerie, cascading exhortation for peace. Intriguing in parts, the mantra continues for almost 12 minutes, sustained by constant feedback. "We finished with Yoko's number because you can't go anywhere after you've reached that sort of pitch," Lennon explained. "And to end the show I just said, 'Look, at the end, when she's finished doing whatever she's doing, just lean your guitars on the amps and let it keep howling, and we can get off like that'." Lennon's instructions were fully heeded, leaving the audience to bathe in a full minute of speaker reverberation before roadie Mal Evans turned off the equipment, ending this memorable exercise in musical spontaneity.

JOHN LENNON/PLASTIC ONO BAND

RELEASED: DECEMBER 1970

[ORIGINAL UK ISSUE: APPLE PCS 7124]

It is intriguing to consider that the most groundbreaking and accomplished album of John Lennon's career might never have happened had he not received a book in the post. The tome in question was *The Primal Scream* written by Arthur Janov, a psychologist who was to have a profound influence on Lennon's thinking in the immediate wake of The Beatles' break-up. With the possible exception of Brian Wilson's mentor Dr Eugene Landy, no psychologist has ever had such a startling effect on a rock performer's writing and musical direction. As soon as Lennon began paging through the book, he realised that the contents were deeply relevant to his troubled situation. He was particularly impressed by the case studies of patients who testified to having discovered a cure for their adult neuroses by belatedly confronting their childhood nightmares.

Janov's theories made exciting reading. He believed in the therapeutic value of regression techniques as an aid to restoring a patient's ability to feel. His central thesis was that man's alienation and inability to form fruitful personal relationships stemmed from infant rejection and childhood trauma. As he explained: "The single most shattering event in the child's life is that moment of icy, cosmic loneliness when he begins to discover that he is not loved for what he is...." What his therapy offered was a systematic removal of the layers of conditioning by which the individual masks his pain. By facing the monsters of his imagination and embracing that primal moment of darkness, the patient could then exorcise the original source of the pain. This catharsis was ultimately realised through the uttering of what Janov called the "primal scream", after which the individual would emerge reborn and ready to enjoy life in a more healthy psychological state.

Lennon was astounded by the implications of the book, which offered the chance to cut through to the very root of his life's problems. He already knew that the traumas he had suffered as a child had left deep scars and unresolved feelings of bitterness. When his parents' marriage had ended, he was eventually faced with the terrible choice of choosing between them. Oscillating in emotional confusion between his father and mother, he finally turned to Julia Lennon, only to be abandoned by her soon after and placed in the loving custody of his aunt. During his adolescence, he re-established a close relationship with his mother Julia, only to lose her again when she was killed in a road accident near his home in July 1958. "He just went to his room into a shell," his Aunt Mimi recalled.

His wayward father, who had lost contact with John over the years, did not reappear until the emergence of Beatlemania. Nor did the pain end there. The sins of the father were repeated in the next generation when John Lennon left his wife Cynthia and son Julian. By his own admission, he had spent little time with the boy and since pairing off with Yoko, regular contact between father and son had all but ceased.

Although the impressionable Lennon still felt the stings of disillusionment following his involvement with the Maharishi Mahesh Yogi, he could not resist the lure of Janov's message. What particularly appealed was the notion that he could unleash a lifetime's neurosis in one great cathartic scream. As he later admitted: "I would never have gone into it if there hadn't been the promise of this scream, this liberating scream."

If John had good reason to feel empathy with Janov's theories then the same could be said of Yoko Ono. Although the daughter of wealthy and successful parents, her upbringing was not without its share of suppressed feelings of rejection. She had not even met her father until the age of two and, for much of her childhood, her mother was an aloof, distant presence. With two broken marriages behind her and her child Kyoko now in the hands of her ex-husband Tony Cox, she seemed another likely Janov case study. What probably clinched the matter was her now stormy relationship with Lennon. While weaning themselves off heroin, their romantic fantasies had been undermined by bickering and domestic tension.

Lennon's aide Anthony Fawcett documented, with notable perception, the seriousness of a marriage in crisis: "Early in 1970, in addition to his despair that The Beatles really were finished, there were mounting tensions in his relationship with Yoko, which became more destructive day by day. He retreated into passivity and inertia... John and Yoko took the only escape they knew from pain and anxiety and hid in each other's love. But rapidly it became an obsessive, possessive love; without realising it they were stifling each other... Living with them became harder by the day... I was acutely aware of the rapid deterioration of their relationship... John escaped from his problems by watching television. It seemed as if he didn't really care where he was as long as there was a colour television at the foot of the bed... John and Yoko isolated themselves, communicating with no-one. In part, I saw their withdrawal as a reaction to the frantic pace of the year before, the continual dialogue with the media, the peace efforts, all the travelling. Also, although he didn't realise it at the time, John desperately needed somebody else to turn to, someone to help him besides Yoko, who acted as his only outlet. It was obvious to me that their relationship could not continue much longer the way it was going."

In March 1970, the Lennons enrolled in Arthur Janov's primal therapy programme. Over the succeeding months, John worked through his childhood pain in search of catharsis. During the therapy, designed to strip him of psychological defences, he could be observed sitting on the floor, rocking back and forth, and screaming like an infant as he tore away at the falsities that blighted his ability to express his true self. "In the therapy you really feel every painful moment of your life," he noted. "It's excruciating. You are forced to realise your own pain, the kind that makes you wake up afraid with your heart pounding."

Despite the rigours of the therapy, Lennon persevered and was astounded by the early effects. "It was the most important thing that happened to me besides meeting Yoko and being born," he gushed. At one point, he got so carried away with the programme's healing properties that he threatened to convert the world. "John was really taken with primal therapy," Janov stressed. "He wanted to rent the *QE2* and have us sail around the world doing primal therapy. He wanted to buy an island and found a primal nation. He was pretty serious. I put the kibosh on it."

After five months with Janov, Lennon was finally obliged to terminate the treatment and concentrate on his ongoing battle with the US immigration authorities, which had already petitioned for his deportation. He had no choice. "He was forced to leave," Janov regretted. "It really botched the whole process."

Despite Janov's understandable regret, the primal therapy sessions were far from worthless or unsuccessful. Lennon emerged not only with a new

attitude, but a head full of remarkable lyrics. Through the summer of 1970, he underwent an inner voyage of discovery, composing an album of songs that were among the finest and certainly most intense of his entire career.

In transferring his ideas on to record, Lennon felt he required minimal embellishment. For the rhythm section, he turned to two old friends, Klaus Voormann and Ringo Starr, who offered a pared-down sound that perfectly complemented the material. Legendary producer Phil Spector was also called upon and his contribution was to attempt precisely the opposite of his early Sixties' wall of sound experiments. Instead of drowning Lennon's voice in Wagnerian orchestration, his job was to ensure that the stark and raw texture of the vocal was captured with perfect fidelity. Yoko, meanwhile, busied herself working on a companion album, which would be released on the same day as her husband's, complete with almost matching cover artwork.

The extraordinary 'John Lennon/Plastic Ono Band' album that emerged from the minute now. So that's what it's all about, just moment by moment. That's how we're living now, but really living like that and cherishing each day, and dreading it too. It might be your last."

I FOUND OUT

Although Lennon would later embrace New York radicals as kindred spirits in his fight for world peace, his attitude towards the counter culture in 1970 was one of evident impatience. Here, his feelings pour out in a vitriolic outburst against the politically hip who dare to pester him on the phone or casually call him "brother, brother, brother, brother". Explaining the genesis of the song to *Rolling Stone*, he complained: "I'm sick of those aggressive hippies or whatever they are, the Now Generation, sort of being very uptight with me, either on the street or anywhere, or on the phone, demanding my attention as if I owed them something. I'm not their fucking parents, that's what it is. They come to the door with a fucking peace symbol and expect to just sort of march around the house or something like an old Beatles fan. They're under a delusion of awareness by having long hair and that's what I'm sick of. I'm sick of them, they frighten me, a lot of uptight maniacs going around wearing fucking peace symbols."

After venting his rage in the first verse, Lennon continues with the hard-edged guitar arrangement to attack all manner of creeds, institutions and belief systems. Eastern and Western religions, macho sexuality and poor parenting are vilified in turn as Lennon catalogues his disillusionment and warns us to be more vigilant and discriminating. Typically, there's a heretical comparison between saviour and pop star, recalling his contro-versial remark about The Beatles being bigger than Christ. Here that contention is restated in the line "I seen religion from Jesus to Paul", with McCartney earning a backhanded compliment in passing. The unrelenting rock rhythm concludes with a couplet that neatly fuses Karl Marx's comments on the opiate of the masses with Janov's beliefs in the therapeutic value of confronting one's demons: "Don't let them fool you with dope and cocaine/Can't do you no harm to feel your own pain".

WORKING CLASS HERO

Lennon extends the theme of 'I Found Out' here to document, with pained ferocity, society's infliction of pain on the individual from the cradle to the grave. It serves both as a song for Everyman and as an intensely personal statement. Indeed, the power of the composition emanates from the subdued, reflective acoustic setting, which conveys a sense of bitter autobiography, as well as offering a sustained denunciation of socialisation, punctuated by swear words omitted from the lyric sheet "at the insistence of EMI". There's a great irony in the song's languid last line, "If you want to be a hero, well just follow me". Far from affirming heroic credentials, the song testifies to the fundamental loss of self that the proletariat suffers in securing societal acceptance and recognition. Explaining his theme to the left-wing journal *Red Mole*, Lennon reflected on the tendency to siphon talent for propagandist effect. "They allowed the blacks to be runners or boxers or entertainers," he pointed out. "That's the choice they allow you – now the outlet is being a pop star, which is really what I'm saying on 'Working Class Hero'... It's the same people who have the power, the class system didn't change one little bit. Of course there are a lot of people walking around with long hair now and some trendy middle class kids in pretty clothes. But nothing changed except that we all dressed up a bit, leaving the same bastards running everything."

In less polemic mode, Lennon saw the song as a thoughtful comment that might appeal to workers, affluent or otherwise. "It's revolutionary," he opined. "I just think its concept is revolutionary and I hope it's for workers and not for tarts and fags... It might just be ignored. I think it's for the people like me who are working class, whatever, upper or lower, who are supposed to be processed into the middle classes, or in through the

love is unbound by time. "I wrote it in the spirit of love," John asserted. "It's for Yoko. It has all that connotation for me and it's a beautiful melody, and I'm not even known for writing melody."

The short lines and three-word aphorisms recall Ono's writing, but there is a crucial difference in Lennon's lyric which is completely devoid of imagery. There's a key moment at the end of both the first and final stanzas of the song during which Lennon defines love as an insatiable infantile hunger for affection ("Love is *wanting* to be loved... Love is *needing* to be loved"). As he pointed out: "The worst pain is that of not being wanted, of realising your parents do not need you in the way you need them. When I was a child I experienced moments of not wanting to see the ugliness, not wanting to see not being wanted."

WELL WELL WELL

Lennon recalls his after-dinner conversations with Yoko during which they discussed such subjects as revolution and women's liberation. The desultory chorus of "well, well, well" sounds suspiciously like a self-deprecating comment on the whole exercise.

Jagged guitar work and a thumping bass drum make this the heaviest and loudest song on the album. Wilfred Mellers described it as a "voodooistic nightmare", citing the line "she looked so beautiful I could eat her" as evidence of a "cannibalistic impulse". Judging from Lennon's lithographs, however, it is more likely that he was referring to the sensual pleasures of oral sex. In this sense, the frantic tribal screams at the close of the song imply orgasmic delight as much as impending violence. It might also be worth noting that in an earlier version of the lyric, Lennon wrote the line, "She looked so beautiful I could wee".

LOOK AT ME

This sweet, reflective, self-questioning ballad sounds strangely out of place amid the intensity of the surrounding material, although it works as a pacific counter-

point. It comes as no surprise to learn that it dates back to pre-primal therapy days, having been previously attempted by Lennon on 'The Beatles' double LP in 1968. The melody recalls 'Julia' from that work, thereby providing another oblique link to Lennon's troubled childhood and mother fixation.

GOD

The climactic moment on the album also proves one of Lennon's most impressive pieces. Phil Spector creates a wide expanse between vocal and instrumentation to add depth to Lennon's meditation, while Billy Preston's Floyd Cramer-style piano serve as a mild sweetener to the secular and spiritual tergiversation.

The opening maxim, "God is a concept/By which we measure/Our pain", is carefully stretched across three lines in order that we savour each and every word. Indeed, Lennon is so struck by the ingenuity of the phrase that he informs us like a pedagogic preacher, "I'll say it again", and proceeds to do precisely that. The emphasis is important, not only because it forces us to concentrate on the hypothesis, but for the way it expresses Lennon's own sense of wonder in conjuring such a conjecture for public consumption. Elaborating on this favourite axiom during an interview with *Rolling Stone*, he postulated: "Pain is the pain we go through all the time. You're born in pain. Pain is what we're in most of the time. And I think the bigger the pain, the more gods we need."

After a short piano interlude, Lennon proceeds to deny every belief system, icon, anti-hero, dictator and cult figure that spills forth from his imagination. The fact that Lennon's litany is an expression of denial rather than an act of devotion makes this anti-prayer even more effective and enlightening. It is only through the extinction of godhead and the realisation of self that he can achieve a sense of redemption.

In explaining the writing of the song, Lennon confirmed that the mantra was very much like a stream of consciousness outpouring produced through word association. "A lot of the words, they just came out of me mouth," he marvelled. "It started off like that. 'God' was stuck together from three songs almost. I had the idea 'God is a concept by which we measure pain', so when you have a word like that you just sit down and sing the first tune that comes into your head and the tune is simple because I like that kind of music... I don't know when I realised I was putting down all these things I didn't believe in. I could have gone on. It was like a Christmas card list. I thought, 'Where do you end? Churchill?... and who have I missed out?'... I thought I had to stop... I was going to leave a gap and say just fill in your own and put whoever you don't believe in. It had just got out of hand."

Significantly, Lennon moved from religious disbeliefs (Buddha, Mantra, Gita) to conclude with the modern day deities of the rock world, notably Elvis and Zimmerman. "I don't believe in Dylan," Lennon added, when interviewed. "I don't believe in Tom Jones either in that way. Zimmerman is his name. My name isn't John Beatle, it's John Lennon."

Saving the best heresy for last, Lennon concluded "I don't believe in Beatles", adding a pregnant pause for dramatic effect. Making this sort of statement in the same year that The Beatles had split was bound to cause speculation. The public had yet to come to terms with the fact that the Fab Four was history but hearing Lennon's emphatic denial of their mythic importance blighted any illusions of a cosy reunion. When questioned on that epochal line, Lennon casually retorted: " I don't believe in The Beatles, that's all. I don't believe in The Beatles' myth. 'I don't believe in Beatles' – there is no other way of saying it, is there? I don't believe in them, whatever they were supposed to be in everybody's head, including our own heads for a period... Beatles was the final thing because it's like I no longer believe in myth, and Beatles is another myth."

After 15 instances of denial, Lennon added a postscript announcing, "I just believe in me", belatedly adding, "Yoko and me", as though she was an extension of himself. "And that's reality", he confirmed.

Even after all this, Lennon still had another shock in store for his listeners. Having denounced The Beatles as mythical entities and affirmed his self-awakening to a new reality, he proceeded to toll the death knell for an entire era. "The dream is over," he announced, and in such an insouciant manner that it was as if it had never mattered in the first place. The myth of the Sixties as expressed through a decade of extravagant headlines, groundbreaking artistic achievements, self-congratulatory hype and youth-conscious idealism was washed away in four short words. "It was a dream," Lennon later insisted. "I don't believe in the dream any more... I don't believe in it, the dream is over. And I'm not just talking about The Beatles, I'm talking about the generation thing. The dream is over. It's over and we've got to – well, I have anyway, personally – get down to so-called reality."

Appropriately, there was no anger or remorse in Lennon's exercise in self-realisation. At the last, he speaks to the listener like a nurse comforting the bereaved with practical advice: "And so dear friends/You'll just have to carry on/The dream is over".

It was a remarkable conclusion to the greatest album of Lennon's career, leaving only the lingering suspicion that there might be more to his faith than the solipsistic "me" or its variant "Yoko and me". It is worth considering some comments from a press conference given not long before he wrote 'God'. Although suitably vague, they hardly attested to an unconditionally atheistic point of view. "I believe that God is like a powerhouse", Lennon suggested, "like where you keep electricity, like a power station. And that He's a supreme power, and that He's neither good nor bad, left, right, black or white. He just is. And we tap that source of power and make of it what we will. Just as electricity can kill people in a chair, or you can light a room with it. I think God *is*."

MY MUMMY'S DEAD

The album's short postscript was this macabre sounding elegy whose tune was borrowed from the nursery rhyme 'Three Blind Mice'. It captures the menace of childhood fears through adult remembrance in a most disturbing fashion. "It was almost like a Haiku poem," Lennon suggested. "Obviously, when you get rid of a whole section of illusion in your mind you're left with great precision. Yoko was showing me some of these Haikus in the original." There is a strong sense of temporal dislocation in the song as Lennon travels back in time to confront the root of his adult neuroses in the form of his mother's death. Like a muted George Formby singing through a megaphone, Lennon expresses in eight terse lines the lingering pain that he could never properly show to the world or vanquish from his psyche.

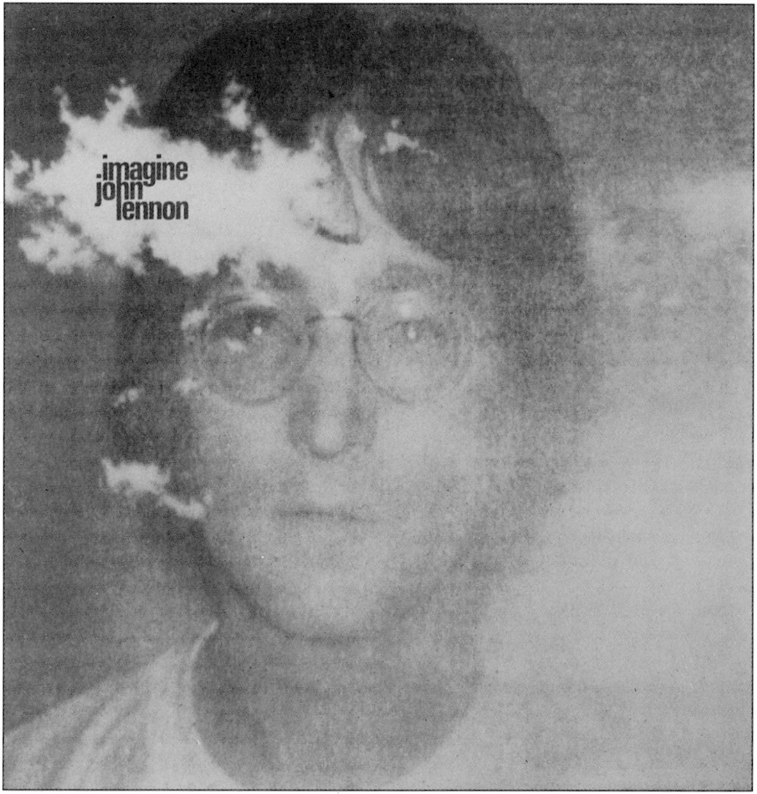
imagine
john
lennon

IMAGINE

RELEASED: OCTOBER 1971

[ORIGINAL UK ISSUE: APPLE SAPCOR 1004]

Although 'John Lennon/Plastic Ono Band' was a commercial success, peaking at number 6 in the US and number 11 in the UK, its sales still lagged behind the first post-Beatles releases of Paul McCartney and George Harrison. Lennon could reasonably claim that he was recording by far the most adventurous material and additionally had allowed his popularity to be compromised by a series of wilfully experimental works with Yoko Ono, which had left potential purchasers suspicious of his product. Whether Lennon felt intimidated by the superior sales of his former colleagues is debatable, but in 1971 he decided to record a more radio-friendly album, aimed directly at the pop masses. In most respects, 'Imagine' was a watered-down version of its predecessor, with a sprinkling of sugared melodies and melodic craftsmanship to make his work a little more palatable for former Beatles lovers.

Four months before the release of this album, McCartney issued his second solo work, 'Ram', which topped the UK charts and spawned a US number 1 single, 'Uncle Albert/Admiral Halsey'. Lennon was appalled by the mediocrity of the material and took surprising offence at several of 'Ram''s innocuous tracks, which he regarded as thinly veiled criticisms of himself, Yoko and the other Beatles. While McCartney had been coy in his criticisms, Lennon was brutally frank, damning his former partner on the devastating character assassination 'How Do You Sleep?' The employment of George Harrison on 'Imagine' and a free photo inside featuring a send-up of the cover of 'Ram' reinforced the attack. With the dispute over Apple having recently been the subject of High Court proceedings, the public was left in no doubt about the enmity between the two leading ex-Beatles.

McCartney offered an olive branch of sorts by praising Lennon's achievement on 'Imagine', while adding "but there was too much political stuff on the other albums". Lennon was unimpressed and responded: "So *you* think 'Imagine' ain't political, it's 'Working Class Hero' with sugar on it for conservatives like yourself!! You obviously didn't *dig the words*... Your politics are very similar to Mary Whitehouse's – saying *nothing* is as loud as saying *something*... Join the Rock Liberation Front before it gets you."

Lennon's arrogance was punctuated by the enormous success of 'Imagine'. Despite a patchy first side, it was a very strong, appealing record, which offered the craft and sumptuous melody missing from his recent, starker work. With the assistance of Phil Spector, Lennon, and The Plastic Ono Band/Flux Fiddlers (basically, George Harrison, King Curtis, Nicky Hopkins and Badfinger's Tom Evans and Joey Molland), the album sounded extremely professional. For those who preferred Lennon's message undiluted by over-sweet melody, it was a little anti-climactic, but how else could he

possibly have followed the brilliant 'John Lennon/Plastic Ono Band'?

'Imagine' fulfilled one crucial objective by re-establishing Lennon with the record buying masses. This time around, he was rewarded by reassuring Beatles sales figures as 'Imagine' topped the charts on both sides of the Atlantic, a statistic which had yet to be achieved, however narrowly, by either McCartney, Harrison or Starr.

IMAGINE

This is undoubtedly Lennon's most famous post-Beatles song, a moving anthem that has come to define the innocent hope for world peace that he propagated during the latter part of his life. Although it was obviously the most crafted melody on the album, its impact was not immediate but grew with generational radio play, reinforced by minor cover versions and a keener public sympathy towards Lennon's quixotic views. In America, the song proved successful as a single, peaking at number 3, but in Lennon's homeland it was only played as an album track until its belated release in 1975. Four years on, its impact was inevitably lessened, although it still rose to an impressive number 6. The chart statistics are a revealing comment on the gradual ascent of the song towards the status of a standard. It was not until after Lennon's murder that the composition finally earned its evergreen status, completing a climb to UK number 1 almost a decade after its first appearance on vinyl.

Along the way, there had been a subtle but significant change in public attitude towards the song, so much so that even some religious groups were not averse to chanting its chorus. Back in 1971, though, the song was not met with universal approbation. Many religious listeners were disturbed that Lennon's imaginary Eden was a paradise without a heaven. In putting society to rights, Lennon envisaged a world without territories or possessions, but his first line of attack was religious beliefs – "Imagine there's no heaven" was the opening line. In interviews Lennon managed to tone down the message, pointing out, "If you can imagine a world at peace, with no denominations of religion – not without religion, but without this 'my God is bigger than your God' thing – then it can be true."

It was not only those sympathetic towards institutionalised religion who felt uncomfortable with 'Imagine'. Radical politicos were unimpressed by Lennon's wishy-washy utopianism, which they felt paraded naïve and palpably unattainable ideals without once suggesting how they might be realised. Lennon had attempted to counter such criticism in advance with the song's humble conclusion, "You may say that I'm a dreamer/But I'm not the only one/I hope someday you'll join us/And the world will be as one". But hadn't Lennon the "dreamer" just told us on his last album "the dream is over"?

Even the public felt some misgivings, which were mainly directed against the bourgeois Lennon pontificating on the dangers of materialism. *Rolling Stone*'s postbag included one letter which sarcastically announced: "Imagine John Lennon with no possessions!" It was a pertinent criticism although, in fairness, Lennon had at least hesitated over the subject of surrendering possessions. Imagining no heaven was "easy if you try"; imagining no countries "isn't hard to do"; imagining no possessions was a more difficult challenge, forcing Lennon to enquire, "I wonder if you can".

The dreamy idealism at the song's core was largely due to the influence of Yoko Ono. Indeed, Lennon was greatly indebted to her poetry for the composition's framework. During the first onslaught of Beatlemania in the spring of 1963, Yoko had published 'Drinking Piece For Orchestra', which opened with the line "Imagine letting a goldfish swim across the sky". Her 'Tunafish Sandwich Piece' from the following year commenced with the words "Imagine one thousand suns in the sky at the same time", while 'Rubber Piece' suggested "Imagine your body spreading rapidly all over the world". While the album's liner notes crediting the sleeve design carefully pointed out "cloud piece on cover by Yoko Ono from *Grapefruit* paperback", there was no mention of any literary contribution to this

song. Never mind that her lyric 'Cloud Piece' featured another key line, "Imagine the clouds dripping..."

Years later, Lennon admitted: "Actually that should be credited as a Lennon/Ono song. A lot of it, the lyric and the concept, came from Yoko. But those days I was a bit more selfish, a bit more macho and I sort of omitted to mention her contribution." He added: "The song was originally inspired by Yoko's book *Grapefruit*. In it are a lot of pieces saying, imagine this, imagine that. Yoko actually helped a lot with the lyrics, but I wasn't man enough to let her have credit for it. I was still selfish enough and unaware enough to sort of take her contribution without acknowledging it. I was still full of wanting my own space after being in a room with the guys all the time, having to share everything."

CRIPPLED INSIDE

In lighter mood, Lennon penned this attack on the spiritual bankruptcy of straight society. Lyrically, it's a simple, unilluminating observation of hypocrisy sung without venom or passion. One musicologist traced the melody back to the days of the black and white minstrels, and there is a touch of music hall frivolity as Nicky Hopkins plays barrelhouse piano, laced with honky tonk styling.

JEALOUS GUY

"I was dreaming of the past", Lennon announces at the beginning of this song, thereby balancing his utopian dreams of the future voiced in 'Imagine'. It's a welcome admission that beneath the idealised love of John and Yoko there lay darker feelings and hidden insecurities. Despite the *mea culpa* tone, the tune is surprisingly jaunty, having been adapted from the composition 'Child Of Nature' which Lennon had written during his visit to India in 1968. There is a similar contrast between high romance and earthy realism in the closing moments of the song where Phil Spector's lavish orchestration clashes head on with Lennon's prosaic, carefree whistling.

The song gained a wider audience in the wake of Lennon's death, when Roxy Music hit the top of the UK charts with their own over-faithful reading.

IT'S SO HARD

Here, Lennon relaxes with a simple blues workout, complete with rocking guitar. Guest artiste King Curtis provides the alto saxophone, while Phil Spector attempts to provide some gloss by incorporating orchestration. It's a pleasant, if unarresting, addition to the album.

I DON'T WANT TO BE A SOLDIER

Musically, this has some interesting shades, with Spector drowning Lennon's vocal in echo, George Harrison providing some impressive slide guitar, Nicky Hopkins adding piano, and King Curtis prompting a short jam towards the end. Alas, the lyrics let the song down. Lennon appears to be emulating 'God', but this is a mantra without a meaning and a lyric with nothing to say. The rhyme scheme (a, a, a, a) merely alternates the words "die", "fly" and "cry", resulting in such banal lines as "I don't wanna be a poor man, mama, I don't wanna fly".

GIMME SOME TRUTH

This passionate rant against hypocrites, pig-headed politicians and chauvinists proves one of the highlights of the album. Lennon's bile pours forth in polysyllabic splendour as he rails against "schizophrenic, egocentric, paranoiac prima donnas". The powerhouse musical backing includes some searing guitar work from Harrison, reinforced by Lennon, and a barrage of drum sound from Alan White. George Harrison's presence is particularly welcome for, in different circumstances, this might have become a Beatles song, having been first attempted in primitive form at the end of one of their sessions back in January 1969.

OH MY LOVE

This beautiful melody again harks back to Beatles' times, having been first attempted as a guitar-based composition in 1968. Musically, the keyboard line dominates, with Lennon on acoustic piano and Nicky Hopkins on electric piano, while Alan White adds some evocative Tibetan cymbals, complemented by Harrison's guitar and some delicate orchestration from Spector. The album's credits diligently note that Yoko Ono is claiming a joint credit for the work, a matter already in dispute with impresario Lew Grade, the new owner of Northern Songs. Reading the lyrics, the Ono influence is self-evident, most notably in the nature imagery, with her familiar references to trees, sky and clouds.

HOW DO YOU SLEEP?

Arguably the highlight of the entire album, this forthright attack on Paul McCartney may have offended some commentators, but it was undoubtedly one of Lennon's most compelling and passionate songs. As he perceptively noted: "It was like Dylan doing 'Like A Rolling Stone', one of his nasty songs, venting my anger or frustration... and using Paul as the object of it." As the documentary film *Imagine* reveals, the studio rehearsal was even more irreverent and vitriolic, with Lennon sneering: "how do you sleep, you cunt?" Although his distant feud with McCartney was raging at the time, the song was more a release for his suppressed spite than a definitive comment on their fragmented friendship. As Lennon explained: "I used my resentment and withdrawing from Paul and The Beatles and the relationship with Paul to write 'How Do You Sleep?' I don't really go around with those thoughts in my head all the time. I wanted to make a funky track and this is a good way to make it."

The song begins with a string section warming up in obvious imitation of the sound of 'Sgt. Pepper's Lonely Hearts Club Band'. So begins the first line of attack on McCartney with the contention, "So 'Sgt. Pepper' took you by surprise".

It's an audacious opening, not least because it seems so blatantly unfair. The underlying suggestion is that Paul was somehow taken aback or even intimidated by The Beatles' or Lennon's artistic progress on that groundbreaking record. Yet, as Lennon certainly knew, the 'Sgt. Pepper' concept was originally McCartney's and he also contributed more songs to the finished product than his accuser. The point is worth making as it indicates Lennon's willingness to interpret events to his rhetorical advantage.

The recent rumours of McCartney's death, the "proof" of which had reached absurd levels of ingenuity from some American quarters, prompts Lennon to conclude: "those freaks was right when they said you was dead". The artistic death that Lennon imagines his partner has suffered since The Beatles' split is only mildly contentious in comparison to the suggestion that he never had any talent in the first place. Taking a line appropriately coined by McCartney's adversary Allen Klein, Lennon derides Paul's artistic contribution to The Beatles, while also taking a cheap shot at his first solo hit single: "The only thing you done was yesterday/And since you've gone you're just another day". This attack is preceded by the suggestion that McCartney is surrounded by sycophants and, apparently worst of all, straight people. Interestingly, it was those last two criticisms that McCartney focused upon in defending his reputation. When asked his reaction to Lennon's gibes, he said: "I think it's silly. So what if I live with straights? I like straights. I have straight babies. It doesn't affect him. He says the only thing I did was 'Yesterday'. He knows that's wrong. He knows and I know it's not true."

Then again, Lennon seemed more than willing to stretch the truth for propagandist purpose. One of the more outlandish lines in the song is Lennon's suggestion that his partner was being hen-pecked ("Jump when your momma tell you anything"). Given Lennon's own reliance on Yoko Ono and the vitriol he had received from the media for allowing her to dominate his life, this seemed a surprisingly cheap shot. Viewing such

sentiments from a more charitable angle, one is tempted to argue that Lennon, ever the self-analyst, is projecting his own feelings outwards. At the time of the album's release, he suggested: "I could have been writing about myself". The tendency to see McCartney as his mirror opposite, a view intensified by years of songwriting, performing and friendship, may have blurred Lennon's vision. Moreover, in recognising McCartney's artistic decline, he must have been aware of his own susceptibility to falling standards now that The Beatles' quality control could no longer be called upon.

By the final verse, his attacks become more pointed as he accuses McCartney of surviving on his pop star looks ("A pretty face may last a year or two"), then dismisses his latest work as mindless "muzak". The song ends with a despairing plea: "You must have learned something in all those years".

The inflammatory lyrics dominate any reading of this song, but special commendation must be given to Phil Spector's sweeping orchestration, which heightens the drama immeasurably. The presence of another Beatle at the session adds to the tension, and when George Harrison lets rip with an invigorating slide solo at the end of the second verse, the stage is set for a gripping conclusion. Lennon saw many of his songs from this period as news despatches from the front of a private war, and never cared that their topical venom might make uneasy listening at a later date. It is regrettable that the subject matter of this composition would preclude its appearance on later media tributes to the singer.

HOW?

The structure of this composition, with its series of rhetorical questions, recalls the stark self-analysis of Lennon's previous album, but the music is richer. Again two pianos dominate, reinforced by a solid backbeat and Spector's atmospheric use of vocal echo. The descending scale is interrupted by dramatic stops as Lennon's questions end in stasis. After three verses and eight long questions,

there is some resolution in the consideration that life is a struggle that has to be endured. But such platitudes are not enough to pacify the songwriter's troubled spirit and the song ends by repeating the key questions voiced in the first stanza.

OH YOKO!

Lennon celebrates the joys of dependent love with this upbeat tribute to his wife. There is a childlike glee in the lyrics as John describes the all-embracing nature of his love and the seeming ubiquity of Ono in every area of his domestic routine. "It was a very popular track," Lennon enthused. "Everybody wanted it as a single, but I was sort of shy and embarrassed, maybe because it didn't represent my image of myself, of the tough, hard-biting rock 'n' roller with the acid tongue." A veritable musical romp, the song has some lovely moments, not least the exuberant piano solo, Spector's falsetto on the chorus, and the playful Dylanesque harmonica break at the end.

LATE CITY EDITION
WEATHER: Congress shall make ...
law respecting an establishment of ...
ligion, or prohibiting the free exerc...
thereof; or abridging the freedom ...
speech, or of the press; or the right ...
the people peaceably to assemble, an...
to petition the Government for a r...
dress of grievances.

Established 1984

Some Time
in New York City

TO KNOW HIM IS TO LOVE HIM
ONO NEWS THAT'S FIT TO PRINT · — There are no birds in Viet-Nam —sez — JOKO PRES

John & Yoko/ Plastic Ono Band

With Elephant's Memory
Plus Invisible Strings

Woman is the Nigger of the World

Lennon/Ono

If she won't be a slave, we
say that she don't love us
If she's real, we say she's
trying to be a man
While putting her down we
pretend that she's above us
Woman is the nigger of the
world ... yes she is
If you don't believe me, take a
look at the one you're with
Woman is the slave of
the slaves
Ah, yeh... better scream
about it.
And then we leave her flat for
being a fat old mother hen
We tell her home is the only
place she should be
Then we complain that she's
too unworldly to be
our friend
Woman is the nigger of the
world ... yes she is
If you don't believe me, take a
look at the one you're with
Woman is the slave to
the slaves
Yeh think about it).

We insult her every day on TV
And wonder why she has no
guts or confidence
When she's young we kill her
will to be free
While telling her not to be so
smart we put her down for
being so dumb

Woman is the nigger of
the world
Yes she is ... think about it
Woman is the nigger of
the world
Think about it ... do
something about it.

We make her paint her
face and dance

Woman is the nigger of
the world
Yes she is ... if you don't
believe me, take a look at
the one you're with
Woman is the slave to
the slaves
Yes she is ... if you believe me,
you better scream about it.

Repeat
We make her paint her
face and dance.
We make her paint her
face and dance.
We make her paint her
face and dance.

SISTERS, O SISTERS

Ono

We lost our green land
We lost our clean air
We lost our true wisdom
And we live in despair

Sisters, O sisters
Lets stand up right now
It's never too late
To start from the start.

Wisdom, O Wisdom
That's what we ask for
And yes, my dear sisters
We must learn to ask.

Middle 8:

Wisdom, O Wisdom
That's what we ask for
That's what we live for now.

Sisters, O sisters
Let's wake up right on
It's never too late
To start from our hearts.

Freedom, O Freedom
That's what we fight for
And yes, my dear sisters
We must learn to fight.

Middle 8:

Freedom, O Freedom
That's what we ask for

That's what we live for now.

Sisters, O sisters
Let's give up no more
It's never too late
To build a new world.

New world, O New world
That's what we live for
And yes, my dear sisters
We must learn to live.

Middle 8:

New world, O New world
That's what we live for
That's what we must learn
to build.

New world, O New world
That's what we live for
That's what we must learn
to build.

ANGELA

Lennon/Ono

Angela, they put you in
prison
Angela, they shot down
your man
Angela, you're one of the
millions of political
prisoners in the world.

Sister, there's a wind that
never dies
Sister, we're breathing
together
Sister, our love and hopes
forever keep
on moving oh so slowly
in the world.

Angela, can you hear the
earth is turning?
Angela, the world
watches you.

Angela, they soon will be
returning to your sisters and
brothers of the world.

Sister, you're still a people
teacher
Sister, your word reaches far
Sister, there's a million
different races but we all
share the same future
in the world.

Chorus:
They gave you sunshine
They gave you sea
They gave you everything but
the jailhouse key.
They gave you coffee
They gave you tea
They gave you everything
but equality.

→ Register to Vote ←

WE'RE ALL WATER

Ono

There may be not much
difference
Between Chairman Mao and
Richard Nixon
If we strip them naked!

There may be not much
difference
Between Marilyn Monroe and
Lenny Bruce
If we check their coffins.

There may be not much
difference
Between White House and
Hall of People
If we count their windows.

There may be not much
difference
Between Raquel Welch and
Jerry Rubin
If we hear their heartbeat.

Chorus:
We're all water from
different rivers
That's why it's so easy to meet
We're all water in this vast,
vast ocean

Someday we'll evaporate
together.

There may be not much
difference
Between Eldridge Cleaver and
Queen of England
If we bottle their tears!

There may be not much
difference
Between Manson and the Po
If we press their smile.

There may be not much
difference
Between Rockefeller and you
If we hear you sing.

There may be not much
difference
Between you and me
If we show our dreams.

Chorus:
We're all water from
different rivers
That's why it's so easy to me
We're all water in this vast,
vast ocean
Someday we'll evaporate
together.

The entire world is a musical divided by the spiritual sin
instrument, the pole of the Earthly music is an echo o
world celestial is intersected this cosmic harmony. It i
where this heavenly choral is relic of heaven—UNKNOW

SOME TIME IN NEW YORK CITY

RELEASED: JUNE 1972 (US) SEPTEMBER 1972 (UK)

[ORIGINAL UK ISSUE: APPLE PCSP 716]

After arriving in New York, the Lennons were embraced by the local radical community, including Jerry Rubin, Abbie Hoffman and street musician David Peel. John and Yoko even joined some of their new friends in the whimsically titled Rock Liberation Front, a group "dedicated to exposing hip capitalist counter-culture rip-offs and politicising rock music and rock artistes". Although they clearly had a lot of fun, much of their time was spent on more serious issues such as fighting City Hall, attending deportation hearings and engaging in immigration and custody battles. As ever with Lennon, the everyday circumstances of his life permeated his music and songwriting. At a time when introspective singer songwriters were in vogue, Lennon was emerging as a cause-seeking protest singer, a species that had been commercially redundant since Dylan waved farewell to the radical left in the mid-Sixties. International rock fans recently accustomed to songs about Yoko, now had to embrace such names as John Sinclair and Angela Davis and, ideally, show some interest in US prison riots, British foreign policy, the IRA and women's liberation. They also had to swallow the promise of a free live album, only to be confronted by a retail price that was substantially higher than expected.

Those grown used to the craftsmanship of 'Imagine' had a rude awakening in the form of backing group Elephant's Memory, a bar band specialising in Chuck Berry riffs and leftish lyrics. It was, of course, most appropriate for Lennon to use a rough bunch of musicians to play his and Yoko's political street poetry, but many critics and a large proportion of record buyers were alienated by the results. Rolling Stone's Stephen Holden described the album as "incipient artistic suicide" and in a lengthy overview complained that the work was essentially puerile propaganda, adding "The tunes are shallow and derivative and the words little more than sloppy nursery rhymes that patronise the issues and individuals they seek to exalt. Only a monomaniacal smugness could allow the Lennons to think that this witless doggerel wouldn't insult the intelligence and feelings of *any* audience." Taking an overview of John and Yoko's career, Holden praised them for their willingness to pursue avant-garde ideas: "Such commitment takes guts. It takes even more guts when you've made it so big that you don't need to take chances to stay on top: The Lennons should be commended for their daring. What is deplorable, however, is the ego-tistical laziness... that allows artistes of such proven stature, who claim to identify with the 'working class hero', to think they can patronise all whom they would call brothers and sisters."

A publishing dispute between Northern Songs and Ono Music over whether Yoko could reasonably be cred-ited as a co-writing partner delayed the album's release in Britain by several

months. By the time it appeared, most UK critics tended to follow the American line, with *Melody Maker* complaining of "glib politicising" not to mention "mind-less over-kill, cheap rhetoric and appallingly bad lyrics".

Potential purchasers needed only to inspect the packaging or read the song titles to realise the extent of Lennon's political dogmatism. The front cover was a pastiche of *The New York Times*, using song titles as headlines and lyrics as news stories. The US version included a postcard depicting the Statue of Liberty raising a clenched fist and a British Army recruitment ad from the pages of *The Sun*, filled in with John Lennon's signa-ture and the words "Fit To Die" scrawled across the page.

While the bad press that the album received was understandable in view of the overbearing didacticism, Lennon ini-tially felt that the work was a stimulating commentary on his experiences in New York. "The songs we wrote and sang are subjects we and most people talk about," he argued. "It was done in a tradition of minstrels – singing reporters – who sang about their times and what was happening." In later years, he looked back at the work with a more jaundiced eye, fully realising its limitations. "It almost ruined us in a way," he reflected. "It became journalism and not poetry. And I basically feel that I'm a poet... I was making an effort to reflect what was going on. Well, it doesn't work like that. It doesn't work as pop music or what I want to do."

Lennon was correct, inasmuch as his topical songs consisted mainly of simplistic sloganeering, but such is the nature of most *agitprop*. What was refreshing and exciting about the album was Lennon's willingness to release a work so out of place in the rock marketplace. In a period where staid studio work was the norm, 'Some Time In New York City' was a brave and uncompromising album that displayed Lennon's egotism and altruism in equal measure. His determination to use Fifties' style musicianship to rugged effect emphasised the wide-eyed innocence and eagerness of a performer who saw himself as a reformer and political protester, seemingly immune to the jibes of an uncaring public. There is much to commend the album and, over two decades on, it stands up far better than any contemporaneous commentator could reasonably have expected. The passion that Lennon felt for specific causes, combined with the energetic, almost punk-like approach of Elephant's Memory, fashioned an album that thoroughly deserves a full-scale critical rehabilitation.

WOMAN IS THE NIGGER OF THE WORLD

When the arts magazine *Nova* interviewed Yoko Ono for their March 1969 issue, she expressed the view that "woman is the nigger of the world". The phrase stuck with John who was determined to transform his partner's feminist slogan into a popular anthem. Like so many things in his life, Lennon rushed to the feminist cause with the zeal of a new convert. The man who had condescendingly put down pushy women in 'Girl' and exercised male proprietorship in 'Run For Your Life' was now atoning for his chauvinist sins. On the record sleeve, the song is illustrated with a picture of a horned devil, slicing a woman's stomach with a knife. The lyrics are equally direct and espouse the need for a change in male attitudes with firm conviction. There is a discernible sense of wonder in Lennon's phrase "Think about it", as he admonishes the listener to consider the inescapable logic of the song's title. The mood is similar to many of the songs on the 'John Lennon/Plastic Ono Band' album, with Lennon pulling away a veil of false conditioning to confront the world's appalling treatment of women. The catalogue of abuse embraces sexism, psychological manipulation and enforced slavery to motherhood. It is not Lennon's polemic that makes the song, however, but the rhetorical attacks on his audience to wake up to the realities around them. Like a father confessor, he demands an acknowledgement of guilt from the listener: "If you don't believe it, take a look at the one you're with". And, in determin-

ing society's blame, he rightly cries for change ("If you believe me, you better scream about it"). The sheer force of Lennon's argument, built around a sparse but effective tune with "invisible strings", results in one of his best ever political songs. Inevitably, the message was something of anathema to critics and public alike in 1972, but challenged head-on the prejudices of a macho-conscious rock world resistant to change. "It was actually the first women's liberation song that went out," Lennon claimed. "It was before Helen Reddy's 'I Am Woman'... It was talked about. It got the message across. The whole story is the title. The lyrics are just a fill-in. I felt the lyrics didn't live up to Yoko's title."

Inevitably, Yoko's aphorism caused concern to sensitive disc jockeys and a ratings-conscious media wary of causing offence. When the song was first performed on television on *The Dick Cavett Show* in May 1972, the host was obliged to voice a disclaimer prior to the broadcast. Lennon countered this by winning the support of Ron Dellums, chairman of the Congressional black caucus, who issued a statement which was read out on Cavett's show. It said: "If you define 'nigger' as someone whose lifestyle is defined by others, whose opportunities are defined by others, whose role in society is defined by others, the good news is you don't have to be black to be a nigger in this society. Most of the people in America are niggers."

With Lennon also appearing favourably in *Ebony* magazine there was no doubting that he had made his point. Unfortunately, this proved insufficient to win the record a Top 40 placing in the US charts, or even a release on single in the UK, where a copyright dispute continued over Lennon/Ono compositions. Although disappointed by the single's lack of airplay ("It was banned in America because you couldn't say 'nigger'"), Lennon felt justly proud of the composition. "It's such a beautiful statement," he enthused. "What she was saying is true. Woman still is the nigger... You can talk about blacks, you can talk about Jews, you can talk about the Third World, you

can talk about everything but underlying the whole thing, under the whole crust of it is the women and beneath them the children."

SISTERS O SISTERS

The tune may be trite, but Lennon clearly enjoys himself playing rock 'n' roll guitar. Phil Spector's influence is noticeable, but he fails to disguise Yoko's uncertain lead singing. In places she sounds like an out-of-tune version of an early Sixties girl group vocalist. The backing group respond to the lyric's rallying cry with a jaunty performance coaxed by Lennon. "I remember that session," John noted, "because Elephant's Memory, all New York kids, were saying they didn't know what reggae was. I was trying to explain to them all. The only lick I knew to teach them was 'The Israelites', that Desmond Dekker thing... If you listen to it, you'll hear me trying to get them to reggae".

ATTICA STATE

On September 13, 1971, prisoners at the Attica Correctional Facility in upstate New York seized 50 hostages as part of a protest. The authorities responded by sending in 1,700 National Guardsmen and by the end of the siege the death toll read 28 prisoners and 10 guards, with 85 wounded. The following month, on the evening of October 9, Lennon and Ono wrote this rousing protest song which firmly pointed the finger at Governor Nelson Rockefeller, who had refused to intervene by negotiating with the prisoners at Attica. "Rockefeller pulled the trigger", Lennon sang, adding to the political rhetoric with some sweeping views on prison reform: "Free all prisoners everywhere... All they need is love and care". The breast-beating lyrics echoed specific lines from several other Lennon songs, including 'Gimme Some Truth', 'Revolution' and 'Give Peace A Chance'.

Emotionally, the song is not as angry as you might expect from the subject matter, while the arrangement is merely of passing interest, with Lennon producing some guitar flourishes reminiscent of late period Beatles.

On December 17, Lennon appeared at a benefit for the prisoners' families staged at the Apollo Theater, Harlem. He continued to promote the song energetically and even took to wearing a badge proclaiming: "Indict Rockefeller For Murder – Attica." The song was performed on both *The Mike Douglas Show* and *The David Frost Show* and on the latter the singer entered a heated debate with the audience. "We're like newspaper men, only we sing about what's going on instead of writing about it," he explained in defence of his political material. "Wait till they kill your son or daughter..." shouted a disgruntled audience member. "We are society," Lennon replied. "We're all responsible for each other. We have to be." Responding to the criticism that he was making martyrs of the dead, Lennon retorted: "We're not glorifying them. This song will come and go, but there will be another Attica tomorrow."

BORN IN A PRISON

Yoko takes another lead vocal on her own composition, in which she reiterates the sentiments of 'Working Class Hero' perceiving life as one long prison sentence. Stan Bronstein's chafing saxophone dominates the piece creating a cocktail-lounge feel, abetted by strings, the overall effect of which sounds musically out of sync with the work of any other major performer of the period. Nevertheless, it provides an interesting musical complement to the other material on the album.

NEW YORK CITY

Here, Lennon transforms a political rant into a rock 'n' roll boogie with considerable success. The mood is exuberant, with a rollicking piano backing, some great tenor sax and a vocal of excited abandonment. The melody sounds like a direct lift from 'The Ballad Of John And Yoko' which is reasonably apt as this is another autobiographical diary. Lennon relates his meeting with street musician David Peel, when they sang 'The Pope Smokes Dope' for startled onlookers. "We got moved on by the police," Lennon proudly recalled. "It was all very wonderful." The narrative also tells of visiting Max's Kansas City, meeting Elephant's Memory, performing at the Apollo and happily discovering that it was possible to live in New York City without being constantly mobbed by the public and press. "In New York, I could walk around, where I still couldn't walk around in London, " Lennon noted. He closes his song of street protest with the remark, "what a bad ass city", demonstrating that he has already swallowed the New York vernacular.

SUNDAY BLOODY SUNDAY

On January 30, 1972, British soldiers shot dead 13 unarmed Catholic men during a demonstration in Derry in protest against internment. The soldiers later claimed that they shot civilians aiming bombs at them, a charge completely unsubstantiated by forensic tests. At the

end of the inquest into the deaths, Derry City coroner Major Hubert O'Neill reached the chilling conclusion: "I say without reservation – it was sheer, unadulterated murder." In the poorer areas of Northern Ireland, Catholic communities rioted, while in the House of Commons the firebrand MP Bernadette Devlin landed a punch on the person of Home Secretary Reginald Maudling. The murders even inflamed moderate opinion in the south of Ireland, prompting a crowd to burn down the British Embassy in Dublin.

The newly politicised John Lennon was soon drawn into the fray. He joined 1,500 marchers in Oxford Street for a demonstration opposing British policies in Northern Ireland and could be seen carrying a placard which read: "For The IRA Against British Imperialism". Proudly proclaiming his Irish roots, Lennon reminded those present that Liverpool was the uncrowned capital of Ireland. Recalling the demonstration, he noted: "The mood of the crowd was a happy one under the circumstances, considering we were all

there to show our sympathy for the 13 people who were mercilessly shot down by British imperialists."

Musically, Lennon's response to the outrage was similarly uncompromising. Alas, the tune left a lot to be desired, while co-writer Yoko's distracting role was to screech "Sunday Bloody Sunday" in the background. What the song lacked in melody was compensated for by Lennon's no doubt unintended polemic humour. At his sneering best, he announced in one verse: "You anglo pigs and scotties/ Sent to colonise the North/You wave your bloody Union Jacks/And you know what it's worth!/How dare you hold to ransom/A people proud and free/Keep Ireland for the Irish/Put the English back to sea".

Shortly before Lennon's Irish songs were released, Paul McCartney had issued the singalong 'Give Ireland Back To The Irish', which was banned by the BBC. Looking at both songs, it's regrettable that the two writers couldn't have somehow combined their talents to produce a decent anthem. While

McCartney's chant sounded simplistic and sentimental, Lennon's sloganeering was crass and confused. In the final verse of 'Sunday Bloody Sunday', Lennon got so carried away with his own angry rhetoric that he called for repatriation from the "concentration camps". The song remains a stirring and salutary comment on the limitations of pop *agitprop*.

Beneath the anti-imperialist gibes, Lennon was really advocating his usual message of waking up the workers to the wonders of socialism. He later complained of the working class: "They're dreaming someone else's dream, it's not even their own. They should realise that the blacks and the Irish are being harassed and repressed and they will be next. As soon as they can start being aware of all that, we can really begin to do something. The workers can start to take over."

LUCK OF THE IRISH

Lennon and Ono's second Irish song on the album originally began as a folk tune and the retention of a flute indicates its

uneasy transition into a more pop genre. The song's sentiments are condescending with Lennon attempting an ironic viewpoint that doesn't quite come off. Witness the chorus: "You should have the luck of the Irish/And you'd wish you was English instead". Structurally, the verses are split between two perspectives, with Yoko presenting a naïve, sentimental view of Eire, complete with asinine references to leprechauns and the Blarney Stone. Lennon counters with a harsher perspective which documents "a thousand years of torture and hunger". In the fifth verse, he asks, with obvious exasperation, "Why the hell are the English there anyway?" He then takes on the mantle of an over-radical Bob Dylan, fusing 'With God On Our Side' and 'Masters Of War' to stress: "... they kill with God on their side!/Blame it all on the kids and the IRA!/As the bastards commit genocide".

It's easy to criticise the lyrics, but overall this is an impressive, if flawed, composition. The idea of juxtaposing verses of naïve sentimentality with alternate stanzas of hard street rhetoric is both clever and effective and elevates the song from the usual limitations of pure sloganeering.

A week after the horror of Bloody Sunday, Lennon sang this song at a demonstration in New York and agreed to donate the royalties from the composition to the Northern Ireland civil rights movement. His views on the IRA were both forthright and ambivalent. "I don't know how I feel about them," he mused, "because I understand why they're doing it and if it's a choice between the IRA and the British Army, I'm with the IRA. But if it's a choice between violence and non-violence, I'm with non-violence. So it's a very delicate line... We ask for the American Irish to wake up to their responsibility in the same way the Jewish people respond to the problems of Israel."

JOHN SINCLAIR

The radical John Sinclair was a beat poet and founder of the magazine, *Guerrilla: A Monthly Newspaper Of Contemporary Kulchur*. He became Minister of Information for the White Panther Party and managed the MC5, whose controversial album 'Kick Out The Jams' brought the rhetoric of the political/musical underground to the mainstream rock community. In 1969, Sinclair was arrested for selling marijuana to an undercover policeman. Although the haul consisted of a mere two joints, Sinclair was sentenced to an outrageous term of 10 years' imprisonment. He had already served two-and-a-half years before the intervention of John Lennon, who attended a "Free John Sinclair" rally at the Chrysler Arena, Ann Arbor on December 10, 1971. The event, which featured Stevie Wonder on the bill, was captured on celluloid, but the film, provisionally titled *Ten For Two*, was never released.

Lennon closed his segment of the show with 'John Sinclair', written specially for the evening. Amazingly, Sinclair was freed within 55 hours of the concert, which testified to the potency of the protest. Prior to the performance, Lennon recorded this studio version of the song, which was subsequently doctored by Phil Spector. Undercover agents from the FBI kept a vigilant eye on Lennon's political and musical activities during this period and one report noted that this track "probably will become a million seller... but it is lacking Lennon's usual standards". Alas, the FBI's resident rock critic failed to appreciate Lennon's wonderful slide guitar work, which provides the song with a musical clout missing from many of the other tracks on this album. Lyrically, it's simple, provocative and thought-provoking with a catchy refrain contrasting the sentence with the offence ("They gave him ten for two") and a grand finale in which Lennon chants "gotta" 15 times before adding "set him free".

ANGELA

Lennon's next campaign concerned black radical Angela Davis, who had supplied firearms which were used by Jonathan Jackson to free his Black Panther brother George Jackson and two associates. During George's trial the younger brother drew a gun, then kidnapped the judge, several jurors and the district attorney. The episode ended in carnage with prison guards besieging a van, resulting in the deaths of the judge and Jonathan Jackson. Angela Davis was subsequently arrested and charged with conspiracy, kidnapping and murder. Lennon and Ono completed this protest while she awaited trial. It's a pleasant melody enhanced by the sheen of Phil Spector's production, with Stan Bronstein's saxophone and Adam Ippolito's organ sound prominent. Yoko takes the lead vocal which is impressive enough, but the lyrics leave much to be desired. They range from the extravagantly momentous ("Angela, you're one of the millions of political prisoners in the world") to the amusingly banal ("They gave you coffee, they gave you tea/They gave you everything but equality").

WE'RE ALL WATER

Yoko takes lead vocal on her third solo composition on the album. The lyrics can be traced back to her 1967 poem 'Water Talk', which contained the aphorisms and pantheistic philosophy discussed in the song. There are also references to

President Nixon and Chairman Mao stripped naked, an idea visualised in a mock-up picture on the album's sleeve. Although the tune is not particularly memorable, the backing is hilarious. Bronstein's rasping sax and Yoko's vocal exclamations combine to create a sound which recreates nothing less than the spirit of Johnny And The Hurricanes. It's a suitable romp with which to close the studio segment of the package.

COLD TURKEY

The bonus album 'Live Jam', began with the two songs featured by The Plastic Ono Band at the UNICEF Benefit, staged at London's Lyceum ballroom on 15 December 1969. "This song's about pain," Lennon announces as his makeshift supergroup, including George Harrison, Eric Clapton, Billy Preston and Keith Moon, tackle the harrowing drug song that The Beatles once rejected. Lennon screams in paroxysms of pain as his players provide a solid unvarying backbeat. As the song progresses, Lennon's voice gets wilder, re-enacting a roar that can be traced back as far as the tonsil-torturing 'Twist And Shout'.

DON'T WORRY KYOKO

What probably mystified audiences in 1969 can now be seen as a stunning finale by a greatly underrated performer. Setting the scene, Yoko emerges from her white bag and announces "John, I love you", then accuses, "Britain, you killed Hanratty, you murderers." Backed by gut-wrenching feedback, she loses herself in the 'Don't Worry Kyoko' mantra, which builds in intensity. As her screams increase in volume, The Plastic Ono Band find an enthralling three-chord groove, reinforced by a counter melody from Delaney And Bonnie's brass section. No punches are pulled as the spectators receive the full Yoko vocal treatment in excess of 17 minutes. Heaven knows what the audience must have made of the evening. What is clear is Lennon's willingness to provide Ono with centre stage for the lion's share of the performance. In this strange and remarkable song, he saw rock's future and was never afraid to express that opinion. "Yoko's whole thing was that scream," he enthused to *Rolling Stone*. "Listen to 'Don't Worry Kyoko'. It's one of the fucking best rock 'n' roll records ever made. Listen to it and play 'Tutti Frutti'. Listen to 'Don't Worry Kyoko'... If somebody with a rock oriented mind can possibly listen to her stuff you'll see what she's doing. It's fantastic. It's as important as anything we ever did. Listen to it and you'll know what she's putting down... She makes music like you've never heard on earth."

WELL (BABY PLEASE DON'T GO)

The second side of the 'Live Jam' featured John and Yoko guesting with Frank Zappa's Mothers Of Invention at the Fillmore East on June 6, 1971. "This is a song I used to sing when I was in the Cavern in Liverpool," John announces. "I haven't done it since, so..." What follows

is the B-side to The Olympics' 1958 US Top 10 hit 'Western Movies', composed by the group's founder Walter Ward. Lennon's lead vocal is exceptionally strong, while Ono uses her screams as backing vocals. Zappa's guitar solo is also impressive, allowing Lennon the freedom to show us his greatness as a rock 'n' roll singer. This fine opening song stands up against anything on the better known 'Rock 'n' Roll' album.

JAMRAG

A screaming session merges with a cacophonous backing and meanders into a jam, with pianist Ian Underwood providing the familiar Zappa flavour. It's very much a case of Yoko meets the Mothers. Although Lennon/Ono take full credit for the piece, the backing appears to be adapted from Zappa and the Mothers' 'King Kong'. But is this section part of 'Jamrag' or the succeeding 'Scumbag'? It is difficult to decide where the Lennons felt 'Jamrag' actually ended on the album. On the inner sleeve the track is timed as 1 minute 50 seconds, although it actually runs for 3 minutes 56 seconds. When Frank Zappa reissued the Fillmore collaboration with the Lennons on his album 'Playground Psychotics', he made no mention of 'Jamrag' but instead transformed the jam into two separate songs, 'Say Please' and 'Aaawk', the credits of which read Lennon/Ono/Zappa.

SCUMBAG

The jam continues as Lennon shouts 'Scumbag'. Again, there is some discrepancy about where this song begins and 'Jamrag' ends. The inner sleeve times 'Scumbag' as 15 minutes which suggests that the Lennons saw the song actually beginning not when Lennon announces 'Scumbag', but much earlier, amid the cacophony of Yoko's wail on 'Jamrag', just before the 'King Kong' section. This would explain why Zappa receives a co-credit for 'Scumbag' while the Lennons alone are credited for what they saw as a two-minute 'Jamrag'. On Zappa's 'Playground Psychotics', 'Scumbag' is

timed at 5 minutes 53 seconds, commencing with Lennon's shouting of the title. Zappa also extends the writing credits to include Howard Kaylan.

The track has its humorous moments, most noticeably when Zappa demands a singalong from the audience. "All you gotta do is sing 'Scumbag'," he suggests, adding sarcastically, "Right on brothers and sisters". Overall, it sounds like an indulgent romp and enjoyable jam, but lacks enduring appeal as a concert memento.

AU

Feedback and electronic effects mesh together as Yoko utters a sound that resembles a deranged wounded animal. On Zappa's 'Playground Psychotics', this track is sarcastically retitled 'A Small Eternity With Yoko Ono'. It's at times painful listening as Yoko takes us into that familiar refrain 'Don't Worry Kyoko', which by now has become something of a personal anthem. It seems as appropriate a way as any to conclude this much underrated and still unfashionable double album.

MIND GAMES

RELEASED: NOVEMBER 1973

[ORIGINAL UK ISSUE: APPLE PCS 7165]

Following the release of 'Some Time In New York City', John and Yoko slimmed down their public appearances, although not before topping the bill at Central Park and Madison Square Garden for the celebrated One To One concerts for mentally handicapped children. These were to be John Lennon's sole full scale shows following the break-up of The Beatles and the last time on which he appeared on stage with Yoko. At one point a live album was scheduled, but it was placed on indefinite hold and would not be salvaged until as late as 1986 for the posthumous release, 'Live In New York'.

With their immigration status increasingly dominating their lives and Yoko still fighting for custody of her daughter, Kyoko, the pair decided to curtail their political activities, although there were fleeting appearances, including a solidarity showing at a demonstration outside the South Vietnamese Embassy in Washington and the launching of a campaign for the reprieve of Michael X. Apart from those, Lennon also attended the Watergate hearings and watched with fascination as the counter-culture's arch nemesis was unmasked before the nation.

For most of this period though, Lennon retreated to the staid daily regulation of apartment life. Creatively, he remained in the artistic doldrums. While Yoko Ono issued the double album 'Approximately Infinite Universe', her most accomplished solo work to date, John hit a dry writing patch, made worse by a singular lack of motivation. "I either write songs or I don't," he blithely explained at the time. "It's getting to be work. It's ruining the music. Every time I strap on a guitar, it's the same old jazz. I just feel like breathing a bit."

Despite these protestations against the work ethic, Lennon felt obligated to do *something* and roused himself sufficiently to enter New York's Record Plant East studio in the hope of completing a new album. Initially the news was encouraging. It transpired that Lennon was abandoning the overt *agitprop* of 'Some Time In New York City' and recording a more orthodox album without assistance from Yoko. Hopes were high for a return to the tuneful craftsmanship of 'Imagine' or, even better, the stark soul searching of 'John Lennon/Plastic Ono Band'.

Unfortunately, the new album proved severely anti-climactic. Most of the songs were written in the weeks prior to the sessions and lacked the depth and quality of his better studio work, without the concomitant merits usually provided by spontaneity. In interviews of the period, Lennon openly revealed that he was far from confident about the album's merits and betrayed a lack of enthusiasm for the project that was worryingly apathetic. Most artistes "talk up" an album on release, but Lennon seemed ready to throw in the towel, as if challenging reviewers to confirm that he was a spent

force. *Melody Maker* gleaned the following information from the world-weary ex-Beatle: "The album's called 'Mind Games' and it's, well, just an album. It's rock 'n' roll at different speeds. It's not a political album, or an introspective album... There's no deep message about it... The only reason I make albums is because you're supposed to."

Although Lennon may have been attempting to shrug off his radicalism in the hope of regaining some of his mainstream audience, his comments testify to an overwhelming disillusionment with the entire music business. At different times, Lennon responded to such feelings with works of cynicism, introspection or lacerating rage. Here, he seemed largely numb to new ideas, an artiste going through the motions, as though under contractual obligation to complete a work that he knew was largely lacklustre. He later described the album as "an interim record between being a manic lunatic and back to being a musician again."

'Mind Games' was not a complete failure. Indeed, the title track clearly showed Lennon at his best and many purchasers must have bought the album on the strength of that song alone. There were several other promising moments on the album, but overall the work seemed disconcertingly half-baked, while the lack of sparkle in the production was noticeable. It was difficult to avoid the conclusion that he had allowed too much filler to clog up the album, amid a general air of apathy. If he had exercised greater quality control and attempted to compose material to equal the power and beauty of the album's title track, then this would surely have been a major release. As it stands, it represents Lennon at his most frustratingly ordinary, an artiste adrift in the early Seventies without an agenda.

Two telling statistics from the period summed up the current state of ex-Beatledom. It was no surprise that Paul McCartney's 'Band On The Run' topped the US/UK charts as the year closed, while Lennon had to be content with US number 9 and UK number 13. What was more revealing was watching Ringo Starr's 'Ringo' outstripping Lennon's

effort on both sides of the Atlantic. With Harrison's 'Living In The Material World' having topped the US charts and climbed to UK number 2 several months before, the figures spoke for themselves. Lennon was now, unarguably, selling less records than any of the other Beatles and, this time around, critics could not blame Yoko Ono or radical politics.

MIND GAMES

Undoubtedly the stand-out track on the album and a fine single as well, this was Lennon at his hippie apotheosis. "Love is the answer", he proclaims in a pointed reaffirmation of the sentiments voiced on 'All You Need Is Love'. Originally, the track was to be titled 'Make Love Not War' but as Lennon explained, "That was such a cliché that you couldn't say it any-more, so I wrote it obscurely. But it's all the same story." In place of the "make love not war" sloganeering, Lennon adds ambitious lines like "putting their soul to the karmic wheel" and speaks of projections into space and time as though he were a science fiction writer. Some of the lyrics were clearly influenced by the prose of Robert Masters and Jean Houston's consciousness-raising book *Mind Games*.

Beneath the surface of the lyrics lies the continuing influence of Yoko Ono. The "mind games" detailed in the song also recall the interaction between John and Yoko during their first meeting at London's Indica Gallery. In the programme notes to her 1967 exhibition *Yoko Plus Me*, Ono recalled their first display of "mind games": "When 'Hammer And Nail' painting was exhibited at Indica Gallery, a person came and asked if it was all right to hammer a nail in the painting. I said it was alright, if he pays five shillings. Instead of paying the five shillings, he asked if it was alright for him to hammer an imaginary nail. That was John Lennon. I thought, 'So I met a guy who plays the same game played'." That same evening Lennon was filmed at the gallery climbing a ladder to read a message on a card through a magnifying glass. It read: "Yes". The singer was strangely impressed by the positive sentiments, which convinced him that Yoko was worthy of his patronage. Now, in the title track of this album, he chose to confirm with emphasis: "*Yes* is the answer".

Musically, 'Mind Games' was among the strongest Lennon tracks of the decade. The lingering influence of Phil Spector is there in that wonderful clash between simple riffs and subtle harmonic changes, creating a delicate imitation of his familiar "wall of sound". As Lennon noted: "That was a fun track because the voice is in stereo and the seeming orchestra on it is just me playing three notes with slide guitar. And the middle eight is reggae. Trying to explain to American musicians what reggae was in 1973 was pretty hard."

When issued as a single, the track climbed to number 26 in the UK and reached number 18 in the US. It deserved to do even better.

TIGHT A$

The pun in the title, complete with pointed typography, was typical Lennon. Here he revisited his rockabilly roots, anticipating the rock 'n' roll album that would be completed at a later date. The vocal is compressed through the use of echo as Lennon attempts to recreate the mood of 'That's All Right Mama'. Sneaky Pete Kleinow, formerly of The Flying Burrito Brothers, provides the steel guitar which takes Lennon to the brink of country rock. Although not the greatest tune, it does provide one of the more interesting moments on an otherwise patchy album.

AISUMASEN (I'M SORRY)

Lennon's humble apology to Yoko Ono mixes a Japanese refrain ("Aisumasen, aisumasen") with an unexpected excursion into the realm of the melancholic alcoholic of country blues. Given Lennon's erratic drunken behaviour at the time, the song certainly sounds like an authentic representation of his confused spirit. The piano of Ken Ascher and a strong guitar break (from Yoko's future paramour David Spinozza) retains listener interest. The tune is borrowed from a previous Lennon composition, 'Call My Name', which was recorded as a home demo in 1971. There's also a reprise of the lyrics to 'I Found Out' ("Can't do you no harm to feel your own pain"), from the Lennon/Plastic Ono Band album, as John cries, "It's hard enough I know to feel your own pain". The result is an occasionally powerful song that brings some depth to the album.

ONE DAY (AT A TIME)

More Yin and Yan stuff from Lennon, presumably directed at Yoko who was about to be replaced in his life by a new companion, May Pang. The lyrics aren't exactly Cole Porter ("I'm the apple and you're the tree... I'm the door and you're the key") as Lennon's analogies all too often fall into comic bathos. By his standards, it's a bland tune with maudlin lyrics sung in an unconvincing falsetto. Despite an uplifting sax break from Michael Brecker towards the end, it fails to enliven.

BRING ON THE
LUCIE (FREEDA PEEPLE)

Fuelled by fears of deportation, Lennon responded to his detractors with this political broadcast. In the first verse, he seems to be imagining a utopia full of immigrants, as well as addressing the US government with the presumptive advice, "Free the people now/Do it, do it, do it, do it, do it now". Writer Jon Weiner, an incisive and revealing commentator on Lennon's political motivations, reckons this "is as political as anything John wrote". Indeed he goes as far as to suggest that Lennon is specifically addressing "...Nixon and his henchmen: as their Watergate crimes were exposed, John reminded them of Vietnam and the blood of the people they killed". The interpretation is provocative, inasmuch as no names are mentioned in the song, beyond some vague references to "paranoia" and an unidentified evil presence ("666 is your name"). But in the political climate of 1973, the lines "As you slip and you slide down the hill/On the blood of the people you killed" would have

struck a chord with radicals while the coy "you were caught with your hands in the kill" (a pun on "till") may well be an oblique reference to Nixon. The following year Neil Young was credited with some similarly vague Nixon bashing when using the phrase "I never knew a man could tell so many lies/He had a different story for every set of eyes" ('Ambulance Blues'), even though he too never identified the subject of those lines when interviewed.

Lyrically, 'Bring On The Lucie' may have been naïve but the same could be said for most of Lennon's political songs. At least here he sounds as exhilarated and committed as the fist-raising rabble-rouser on 'Power To The People'. Musically the backing track recalls George Harrison's 'My Sweet Lord' via The Chiffons' 'He's So Fine' with some appealing steel guitar from Sneaky Pete.

NUTOPIAN INTERNATIONAL ANTHEM

The first half of the album closes with the shortest track in the Lennon canon: three seconds of silence, no less. This was the second occasion on which Lennon had used silence as an artistic expression, having previously dealt with the concept at greater length on 'Two Minutes Silence' from 'Life With The Lions'. The idea of a Nutopian International Anthem without a sound was appropriate, in as much as the Greek word for Utopia literally means "nowhere" or "no place". Nutopia, like Thomas More's *Utopia*, is an unrealizable ideal, but rather fun to imagine. It was typical of John and Yoko to respond to the realities of deportation not merely by campaigning publicly but by escaping into the sanctuary of their own imaginations. Pressed by the hard hand of officialdom, they called a press conference at which the Declaration of Nutopia (reprinted on the album sleeve) was read. Its whimsical conceit was mildly amusing: "We announce the birth of a conceptual country, NUTOPIA. Citizenship of the country can be obtained by declaration of your awareness of NUTOPIA. NUTOPIA has no land, no boundaries, no passports, only people. NUTOPIA has no laws other than cosmic. All people of NUTOPIA are ambassadors of the country. As two ambassadors of NUTOPIA, we ask for diplomatic immunity and recognition in the United Nations of our country and its people." The notion of a "conceptual country" owed much to Yoko Ono's conceptual art which required a similar leap of the imagination on the part of the viewer, while the "nutopian" sentiments echoed Lennon's daydream theories in 'Imagine'.

INTUITION

This love song to music and the power of intuition is let down by an unmemorable melody, set against an ersatz ragtime arrangement. Pleasant but insubstantial, it sounds suspiciously like a filler on an album that urgently needs a higher ratio of strong songs.

OUT THE BLUE

Following an acoustic opening, the song offers slices of gospel, country and choral. Lyrically, Lennon switches uneasily from gruesome metaphor ("All my life's been a long slow knife") to a wacky simile ("Like a UFO you came to me/And blew away life's misery"). Despite some good ideas, the composition sounds very much like a song idea that has not been fully developed. Like other material on the album it gives the strong impression of work completed rapidly to order.

ONLY PEOPLE

A song of optimism which recalled both Ono's adage "Only people can change the world" and Lennon's mantra "Nothing's gonna change my world" (from 'Across The Universe'). Unfortunately, the "right on" lyrics sound terribly dated, with Lennon proclaiming to his followers, "We don't want no pig brother scene!" Similarly, the sound is very much like mainstream studio rock of the early to mid-Seventies and is largely devoid of Lennon's distinctive imprint and musical edge.

I KNOW (I KNOW)

This reflective acoustic ballad proved one of the better songs on the album. The emotional commitment, largely missing from the other songs he recorded during this period, is clearly revealed here. More than simply a love song to Yoko, the composition testifies to Lennon's own vulnerability and insecurities in a series of convoluted lines. There's an acceptance of passing time and emerging wisdom ("I am only learning/To tell the trees from wood") ending in the same conclusion as 'God' that the only reality is belief in himself and Yoko ("As we share in each other's minds").

YOU ARE HERE

Building on the John and Yoko myth, this attempts a spiritual fusion of East and West, as Lennon brings together the two cities of Liverpool and Tokyo in the grand symbol of his immemorial, romantic love. The steel guitar dominates, adding a Hawaiian air to the proceedings.

MEAT CITY

The album ends with this playfully acerbic and thankfully rocky finale. Set against a stirring arrangement, with plenty of guitar, Lennon offers a parody of jive talking with a satirical view of American consumerism gone mad: "Freak City/Chickinsuckin mothertruckin Meat City shookdown USA/Pig Meat City". In the final verse there's a surprise shift of place from West to East as he announces: "Well I'm gonna China to see for myself". The lyric inspires fond memories of The Beatles' 'Back In The USSR', albeit minus that song's wit, attractive melody or inspired arrangement. So ends a frustratingly erratic album which would surely have been better if only Lennon had been more discriminating in his choice of material.

John Lennon June 1952 AGE 11

Walls and Bridges

to mimi

WALLS AND BRIDGES

RELEASED: OCTOBER 1974

[ORIGINAL UK ISSUE: APPLE PCTC 254]

While considering a follow-up to the largely disappointing 'Mind Games', Lennon became deeply involved in a publishing dispute which was to have serious repercussions on his recording schedule for the best part of two years. Morris Levy, one of the most voracious collectors of US artistes' copyrights, owned many of the classic rock 'n' roll hits of the Fifties, including the Chuck Berry standard 'You Can't Catch Me', the melody of which Lennon had borrowed for The Beatles' 'Come Together'. When Lennon admitted plagiarising the tune in an interview, Levy commenced a lawsuit, seeking damages for the unlawful appropriation. Rather than fighting the action, Lennon agreed to record three tunes owned by Levy's publishing company Big Seven for his next album.

The prospect of three rock 'n' roll songs on a Lennon album would most probably have provoked accusations of artistic atrophy, especially coming in the wake of 'Mind Games'. However, if Lennon went ahead with a complete album of cover songs, he could claim that the work was a special edition and a fully realised concept in itself. Other artistes of the era, most notably David Bowie, had released an LP of tributes to their favourite songs and enjoyed considerable success. With no prospect of progressing musically with his present output, a rock 'n' roll album would provide a happy distraction and possibly rekindle his creative fire.

Lennon had always loved playing rock 'n' roll material. Even his return to the stage with the Plastic Ono Band had taken place at a rock 'n' roll festival in Toronto. "I like rock 'n' roll, man," he had insisted. "I don't like much else. That's the music that inspired me to play music. There is nothing conceptually better than rock 'n' roll. No group, be it Beatles,

Dylan or Stones has improved on 'Whole Lot Of Shakin'' for my money."

Although Lennon would not be recording Jerry Lee Lewis material, he had enough classic songs in mind to begin the covers project in earnest. In order to create an authentic Fifties' sound, Lennon placed himself in the hands of Phil Spector, who was given full artistic control of the sessions, which took place at the end of 1973.

What seemed an excellent idea subsequently backfired when the increasingly erratic Spector absconded with the session tapes. Months passed and, with no news forthcoming from Spector, Lennon decided to abandon the project and write some new songs. He had just entered the recording studio to work on a new album when the Spector tapes were belatedly retrieved. When Lennon played them back he was shocked by some of his drunken performances and, worse still, realised that Spector's "wall of sound" method of recording meant that the worst moments could not be isolated and wiped.

Rather than re-record the songs from scratch, Lennon preferred to forget Phil Spector, Morris Levy and rock 'n' roll and forge ahead with his new work. The title 'Walls And Bridges' was inspired by a phrase he heard on television one evening. In Lennon's mind, it was symbolic: walls suggested protection, bridges offered escape. And anybody who had witnessed Lennon's life over the previous year could testify to his entrapment between both states. He had split with Yoko Ono and moved to Los Angeles to pursue and suffer what he later described as his "lost weekend". The separation was a mysteriously calculated affair masterminded by Yoko, who had even provided John with a companion, her assistant May Pang. "Her coolness shocked me," May Pang wrote of Yoko's decision. "I was hurt by the ease with which she was trying to hand over her husband. I couldn't believe this was happening to me."

Once in LA, Lennon swiftly hit a downward spiral, drinking frequently and playing the boorish rock star in public.

Tales of his wayward exploits filled gossip columns and, with fellow drinker Harry Nilsson egging him on, Lennon soon became a *cause célèbre*. As he pithily noted: "So I was drunk. When it's Errol Flynn, the showbiz writers say, 'Those were the days when men were men'. When I do it, I'm a bum."

Even as a bum, Lennon was still surprisingly creative. He produced an album for Nilsson and soon turned the darker moments of his lost weekend into a series of songs which were most impressive. Instead of the desultory material that had weakened 'Mind Games', Lennon found himself penning some of his best work of the decade. He recoiled in disbelief at his unlikely ability to forge such a well-crafted and consistent record amid the chaos of his personal life. "I'm almost amazed that I could get anything out," he later admitted. "But I enjoyed doing 'Walls And Bridges' and it wasn't hard when I had the whole thing to go into the studio and do it... I'm just glad that something came out. It's describing the year, in a way, but it's not as sort of schizophrenic as the year really was."

Confronting his confused relationship with both Yoko Ono and May Pang, Lennon produced an album of contrasting emotional moods, which made fascinating listening. Musically, it was a varied collection, which leant heavily on horn arrangements and revealed a strong affiliation with current trends in black music. Even the artwork was alluring, with a cover featuring paintings from John aged 11. The record was accompanied by a lavish booklet, which included lyrics, more paintings and a genealogy detailing Lennon's Irish roots and tracing back his family tree to such illustrious predecessors as John Lennon (1768-1846), a sailor famous for his daring feats, and John Brown Lennon, a 19th century American labour leader.

With Lennon sales slipping since the glory days of 'Imagine', there was no guarantee that 'Walls And Bridges' would win back a mass audience. All that changed in December 1974 when the album and attendant single 'Whatever Gets You Thru The Night' both reached number 1 in the US charts.

GOING DOWN ON LOVE

The album opens with a polished, insistent composition, most notable for Lennon's strident vocal and strong horn arrangements from Bobby Keys and friends. Essentially it's a song of loss, with Lennon despairing, "I'm drowning in a sea of hatred". Yet there is the feeling that he protests too much, a view compounded by the jaunty tone of the piece. While the lyrics suggest submission, the entire execution of the song is irreverent and defiant.

WHATEVER GETS YOU THRU THE NIGHT

Bobby Keys' tenor saxophone again dominates as Lennon lets rip with this catchy rocker, which also features Elton John on backing vocals. As Lennon explained: "How that record came about was that Elton was in town and I was doing it and needed a harmony. He did the harmony on that and a couple more and played beautiful piano on it. Jokingly, he was telling me he was going to do this Madison Square Garden concert and

he said, 'Will you do it with me if the record's number 1?'" When the record unexpectedly topped the US charts, Elton called in that promise and John appeared before an audience of 20,000 at Madison Square Garden on 28 November 1974.

Despite the enormous success of this collaboration, Lennon felt its chart position was undeserved. "That was a novelty record." he complained. "It's the only one I've done since I left The Beatles to get to number 1. We didn't get a good take on the musicians, but I just quite like the words. It was more commercial than, say, 'Imagine', but in my opinion. 'Imagine' should have been number 1 and 'Whatever Gets You Thru The Night' should have been number 39. It just doesn't make sense. Who knows?"

Lennon's positive comments on the lyrics emphasise a feature of the song not usually appreciated. There is a touch of Yoko Ono imagery in the line "Don't need a sword to cut through flowers", while the overall mood of the track is triumphantly stoical. He would later claim that he was spiritually lost during this period, yet here he sounds defiantly happy with his lot.

OLD DIRT ROAD

In common with parts of 'Imagine', two pianos are used here, with Lennon playing alongside Nicky Hopkins. Co-writer Nilsson appears as backing vocalist and Jesse Ed Davis adds the country-style guitar. Again the dominant mood is stoical rather than despairing with Lennon's *laissez-faire* lyrics including some pretty interesting imagery: "Trying to shovel smoke with a pitchfork in the wind".

WHAT YOU GOT

Funky rhythms, scorching vocals and belting brass characterise this track in which Lennon attempts a marriage between Sly Stone, The Isley Brothers and early Tamla Motown. Lyrically, this could be the theme song for Lennon's lost weekend as he bemoans the absence of Yoko ("You don't know what you got until you lose it") before imploring "Give me one more chance". Although the party atmosphere suggests one long drinking binge, neither the musicianship nor the arrangement is noticeably slack.

On the contrary, this song sounds much better than most of the material on 'Mind Games', when Lennon was supposedly more in control.

BLESS YOU

One of the most striking melodies on the album, this love song to Yoko adds fuel to the romantic notion that their separation was never intended to be permanent. Part of the song is directed towards the suitor who has replaced Lennon ("Bless you wherever you are/Holding her now..."), but beneath the nobility there is an air of defiance. At one point, Lennon turns on those critics who have already consigned his relationship with Yoko to the history books: "Some people say it's over/Now that we have spread our wings/But we know better darling". Ken Ascher's electric piano and mellotron playing adds a supperclub glitz to the track, as Lennon insists "Now and forever our love will remain". The composition remains one of his most prophetic and convincing love songs.

SCARED

This track begins with the sound of a howling wolf as Lennon relates his fears, which consist largely of encroaching age, passing time and lost opportunities. The mood though is less maudlin than stoic, with the singer concluding: "It is what it is". Backed by some bluesy horn playing, Lennon's vocals become more passionate as he screams, "Hatred and jealousy gonna be the death of me". The examination of his darker side culminates in the revealing couplet, "Sing about love and peace/Don't wanna see the red raw meat". Here, he tears away the familiar Lennon persona of the past few years, ridiculing his "love and peace" philosophy and confronting the red meat of human emotion that is gnawing at his heart. It is a powerful statement and proof positive that the pain of his separation from Yoko could work to his artistic advantage.

"I was terrified when I wrote it, if you can't tell," he recalled. "It was the whole separation from Yoko, thinking I lost the one thing I knew I needed. You know, I think Mick Jagger took the song and turned it into 'Miss You'. When I was in the studio, the engineer said: 'This is a hit song if you just do it faster'. He was right because 'Miss You' is a fast version of my song. I like Mick's record better. I have no ill feelings about it. It could have been subconscious on Mick's part, or conscious. Music is everybody's possession. It's only music publishers who think that people own it."

9 DREAM

One of the highlights of the album, this sumptuous, Spectoresque production displayed Lennon's love of great melody to excellent effect. The velvet vocal and whispered backing from May Pang is spine-tingling stuff and it was no surprise when this track was selected as a single.

"That's what I call craftsmanship writing," Lennon explained, "meaning I just churned that out. I'm not putting it down, it's just what it is. I just sat down and wrote it with no inspiration, based on a dream I had... I wrote it around the string arrangement I'd written for Harry

Nilsson's album I produced. 'Many Rivers To Cross', the Jimmy Cliff number. I'd done this string arrangement for that and it was such a nice melody on the strings... So I just wrote words to the string arrangement, that was '# 9', kind of psychedelic, dreamy kind of thing."

Jesse Ed Davis' guitar playing on this track has been compared with that of George Harrison and it may be that Lennon was attempting to pay passing tribute to his former colleague. Listen closely and you can hear May Pang intoning the word "Krishna" in the background.

SURPRISE SURPRISE (SWEET BIRD OF PARADOX)

With Elton John on harmony, Lennon offers a love song, clearly directed at May Pang. The sentiments are hardly romantic though, as Lennon hints that the relationship is merely functional and probably temporary: "She gets me thru this God awful loneliness". There is even a suggestion that May Pang, although a positive influence on his libido, somehow deadens his true feelings: "She makes me sweat and forget who I am". The bracketed subtitle, ostensibly a throwaway pun on "sweet bird of paradise", nevertheless hints at the paradoxical nature of his feelings for his new love, who seems needed and used in equal measure. In a more playful mood, Lennon closes the song with phrasing borrowed from the fade-out of The Beatles' 'Drive My Car', significantly one of their most anti-romantic compositions.

STEEL AND GLASS

The playfulness continues in the opening line to this song as Lennon chuckles, then teases the listener with the clue: "This is about your friend and mine?" as off-stage whispers hiss, "Who is it?" The question remains unanswered in the song, although most critics credit Allen Klein as the unlucky recipient of Lennon's wrath. As ever with Lennon's accusative songs, the sentiments can all too easily be turned inwards (witness the line "Your mother left you when you were small", which could apply to both Klein and Lennon). With orchestration recalling the equally vituperative 'How Do You Sleep?', Lennon spits out a series of cheap insults, which are just vague enough to preclude litigation. Although the track is impressive and stands among the best on this album, the bile sounds contrived in comparison to the genuine hurt evident on the more convincing 'How Do You Sleep?' A starker version of 'Steel And Glass' would later be unearthed for the posthumous Lennon album, 'Menlove Avenue'.

BEEF JERKY

This funky instrumental workout, based around a blues progression during the session for '# 9 Dream', features some fine interplaying guitar between Lennon and Jesse Ed Davis. The Little Big Horns, featuring Bobby Keys, provide a neat approximation of Stax soul, sounding not unlike the Mar-Keys or Bar-Kays.

NOBODY LOVES YOU WHEN YOU'RE DOWN AND OUT

Lennon approaches world-weariness on this bluesy lament. "I had been sitting on the song because I knew I would ruin it if I tried to record it at the time I wrote it," he explained. "My head wasn't together to deal with it so I just kept it in my pocket." What finally emerged was another song that seemed to comment on the hollowness of his sabbatical "lost weekend" in Los Angeles. Mid-way through the song, he expresses his disillusionment with the star circus by announcing, "All I can tell you is it's all showbiz". There are tempo shifts in the song as Lennon wrestles himself from the apathy of his situation to cry out in a sudden burst of emotion: "Well I get up in the morning and I'm looking in the mirror to see, ooo wee!/Then I'm lying in the darkness and I know I can't get to sleep, ooo wee!" The sentiments, at once desperate, sarcastic and full of self-loathing, lead to the cynical conclusion: "Everybody loves you when you're six foot in the ground".

"Well, that says the whole story,"

Lennon summed up. "That exactly expressed the whole period I was apart from Yoko. I always imagined Sinatra singing that one. I don't know why. It's kind of Sinatraesque. He could do a perfect job with it. Are you listening, Frank? You need a song that isn't a piece of nothing. Here's one for you. The horn arrangements, everything's made for you. But don't ask me to produce it!"

Sinatra never did record the song but its lyrics obviously appealed to the appeal judge in the subsequent Morris Levy case. Quoting the lines, "Everybody's hustling for a buck and a dime", he pointed out: "The words of John Lennon are an appropriate introduction to this case, which involves alleged broken promises and acrimony between supposed friends in the record industry".

YA YA

In a vain attempt to pacify the litigious wrath of Morris Levy, Lennon included this throwaway version of Lee Dorsey's hit at the end of the album. With 11-year-old Julian Lennon on drums, the track was a brief, hilarious coda, which sounded like it had been recorded in a bathroom. "It was a contractual obligation to Morris Levy," Lennon admitted. "It was a humiliation, and I regret having to be in that position, but I did it. That's the way it turned out. Julian was playing the drums and I just left on the piano and sang, 'Ya ya'."

Levy failed to appreciate Lennon's humour and was not content with the share of publishing royalties received from the song's inclusion at the end of the album. As a result, the track would reappear in more sophisticated form on Lennon's next release.

ROCK 'N' ROLL

RELEASED: FEBRUARY 1975

[ORIGINAL UK ISSUE: APPLE PCS 7169]

The litigious Morris Levy was never likely to be satisfied with a couple of minutes of 'Ya Ya' from 'Walls And Bridges' and soon made it clear that he would be suing Lennon for reneging on his promise to record three songs owned by his publishing company. Aware of Levy's legendary Mafia connections and hard man reputation, Lennon soon realised that he would not be easily fobbed off. A meeting was arranged at which Lennon poured out a persuasive list of excuses for his failure to meet the recording deadline. He blamed Spector for running off with the tapes, related salty tales of drunken antics in the studio, and insisted that the final product was incomplete and so appalling that it could not possibly be released. Levy listened patiently, then pressed Lennon for a solution. The singer was evasive and later admitted: "All I was interested in saying was what I had to say about the tapes. I was very nervous, because I did not know the man and I heard he was annoyed at me. So I told him, as best I could, all about the Phil Spector tapes and what had happened: 'I am sorry you didn't get what you were supposed to get, but this is why'. I explained that for about three-quarters of an hour, or an hour. And he said something like, 'Well that is all very well and good, but I am out of pocket'. And he started writing some figures down on a bit of paper. I don't know what they were, maybe $250,000 or something. I could not follow the reasoning, but if he thought he was out pocket, he was out of pocket as far as I could see."

In the end it was Levy who came up with an ingenious compromise. He suggested that Lennon should complete the rock 'n' roll album and license the work to his television mail order company Adam VIII. The legality of such an agreement would be highly questionable, but Lennon "the television addict" was intrigued by the possibilities. "I was thinking perhaps I could put it straight on TV and avoid the critics and avoid going through the usual channels," he later testified. Bamboozled by Levy's optimistic figures and promises of making a financial killing, Lennon was intoxicated with the idea of creating history as the first major artiste to offer new product exclusively through television mail order. At that moment, Levy convinced himself that he had secured a verbal agreement from Lennon, although nothing was ever committed to paper and the whole mail order concept seemed little more than a fanciful idea that still needed careful negotiation, not least with EMI and Capitol Records.

Urged on by Levy, Lennon rushed the project through, salvaging the best of the Spector material and re-recording the rest at the Record Plant in New York with assistance from the musicians used on 'Walls And Bridges'. In early November 1974, Levy asked for a copy of the completed tapes and John despatched two reels, comprising early rough mixes of all the material. Soon after, under pressure from Lennon's lawyer, Levy provided a breakdown of estimated costs, confirm-

ing that the album would be marketed at a bargain price of $4.98. After all the deductions had been calculated, it was evident that neither Lennon nor Capitol would make much money from the release, which seemed patently unworkable. An impasse was reached but Levy was in no mood to back down and recklessly went ahead with the project.

On February 8, advertisements appeared on American television for an album titled 'Roots'. The package featured an out of date, out of focus photo of

Lennon set against a garish yellow cover bearing the slogan: "John Lennon Sings The Great Rock & Roll Hits". On the back cover there were even a couple of ads for two Adam VIII soul compilations: 'Soul Train Super Tracks' and '20 Solid Gold Hits'. The artwork looked shoddy, the pressing lacked even writers' credits for the individual songs, and the sound resembled that of a glorified bootleg.

Capitol wasted no time in issuing their own official album of the sessions titled 'Rock 'n' Roll'. In order to scupper Levy's promotion, they wired radio stations, television companies and pressing plants threatening legal action. The tactic worked and it was later estimated that Levy sold a mere 1,270 albums, although that figure may have been deliberately downgraded in view of the court proceedings that followed.

Levy attempted to sue Lennon and Capitol for $42 million for breach of contract and damages, but that fanciful figure was soon beaten down. Instead, Levy's Big Seven publishing company was granted a derisory $6,795, while a counter suit from Lennon netted $144,700 damages. Outside the court, Lennon announced: "The reason I fought this was to discourage ridiculous suits like this. They didn't think I'd show up or that I'd fight it. They thought I'd just settle, but I won't." Unsurprisingly, the much maligned *Roots* became a valuable collectors' item, not least because it featured two songs that were not included on the Capitol/EMI release: a cover of Rosie And The Originals' 'Angel Baby' and a histrionic reading of The Ronettes' 'Be My Baby'.

The official 'Rock 'n' Roll' was superior in every respect, boasting a wonderful cover featuring a sneering leather-clad Lennon standing in a Hamburg doorway back in 1961. Musically, the album proved a welcome diversion, enabling Lennon to return to the pre-Beatles days and perform the songs that had inspired him to greatness. His determination to imitate, as closely as possible, the vocal styles and instrumentation of the originals was endearing, but also limiting. On the better known songs, he merely inclines the listener to return to the originals in order to hear a superior performance. The work proved a modest success, climbing to number 6 in both the US and UK charts. For most listeners, it was probably appreciated as an aperitif to Lennon's next album of new material. Who would have guessed that his return to rock 'n' roll roots was actually the prelude to a career retirement that would remain unbroken for the remainder of the decade?

BE-BOP-A-LULA

Lennon starts the album with a faithful copy of Gene Vincent's classic, including a decent imitation of the Virginian's distinctive vocal phrasing. Inevitably, it lacks the period charm of the original which seems far too familiar to warrant a Xeroxed cover version. For Lennon, of course, the Vincent tune had deep significance. "There's a picture on stage with the group before Paul had joined and I'm in a white jacket," he recalled. "That was the day, the first day I sang 'Be-Bop-A-Lula' at

a church fete with The Quarrymen. It was the day I met Paul and he was in the audience, a mutual friend had brought him."

STAND BY ME

One of the undisputed highlights of the album, this version of Ben E. King's 1961 hit was subsequently chosen as a single and graced the US Top 20. Lennon's acoustic strumming leads into a powerhouse production, featuring his most confident and expressive vocal on the album, plus some pleasing slide guitar.

MEDLEY: READY TEDDY/RIP IT UP

A Little Richard medley for the album was not particularly surprising, as the artiste had headlined over The Beatles in Liverpool, back in 1962. On early Beatles' recordings, McCartney had sung Little Richard covers, most notably 'Long Tall Sally', and the raving 'Kansas City' on 'Beatles For Sale'. Here, Lennon gets a belated opportunity to sing lead on 'Rip It Up', which segues nicely into 'Ready Teddy'.

YOU CAN'T CATCH ME

This was the song that prompted Morris Levy's suit for plagiarism against Lennon. With Spector at the controls, the sound is deeply compressed as Lennon provides an atmospheric opening that makes no attempt to disguise the song's relation to The Beatles' 'Come Together'. In interviews, Lennon was always ready to admit his debt to Chuck Berry as a key influence on his musical career.

"Chuck Berry's lyrics were intelligent," he noted. "In the Fifties, when people were singing about virtually nothing, he was writing social comment, songs with incredible meter to the lyrics, which influenced Dylan, me, and many other people."

AIN'T THAT A SHAME

A Top 10 US hit for Fats Domino in 1955 and a number 1 that same year for Pat Boone, this song held special significance for Lennon.

"'Ain't That A Shame' was the first rock 'n' roll song I ever learned," he told journalist Chet Flippo. "My mother taught it to me on the banjo before I learned the guitar." It's a faithful reading of the song, with saxophone dominant and Lennon hamming up the vocal on the chorus.

DO YOU WANT TO DANCE

Bobby Freeman's 1958 hit 'Do You Wanna Dance' had already spawned several chart successes, from The Beach Boys and Bette Midler in the USA to Cliff Richard and Barry Blue in the UK. It was therefore rather too well covered to warrant yet another version. Lennon's reading sounds weary and over-familiar despite an attempt to add a reggae rhythm.

SWEET LITTLE SIXTEEN

Lennon had already rehearsed Chuck Berry's 'Thirty Days' for the album, but stuck to this familiar classic, which he took at a slightly slower tempo and embellished with horns. This was the second of four songs retrieved from the original Spector tapes and reinvested with a fresh vocal. Lennon had no hesitation about recording two Berry songs for the album. "When I hear good rock, the calibre of Chuck Berry, I just fall apart," he confessed. "I have no other interest in life. The world could be ending and I wouldn't care."

SLIPPIN' AND SLIDIN'

Having already recorded Little Richard's 1956 hit 'Long Tall Sally' with The Beatles, Lennon decided to tackle its B-side. It's a rousing vocal performance, although Lennon would be the first to admit that, in common with many of the songs on the album, it pales in comparison with the original. "It was a song I knew," he casually observed. "It was easier to do songs that I knew than trying to learn something from scratch."

PEGGY SUE

One of the first songs Lennon learned to play on guitar was The Crickets' 'That'll Be The Day', a number that was rehearsed for this album but not recorded at the session. The Beatles loved Buddy Holly songs, of course, and dutifully included 'Words Of Love' on 'Beatles For Sale'. Here, Lennon tackles 'Peggy Sue' in as faithful a version as modern technology allows. As well as the familiar lead guitar breaks and primitive percussion, there's a chance to hear John attempting Holly's hiccuping vocal style, which is quite amusing.

MEDLEY: BRING IT ON HOME TO ME/SEND ME SOME LOVIN'

Lennon offers a short medley of two Sam Cooke hits. 'Send Me Some Lovin'' (co-written by Lloyd Price) was familiar to Lennon from earlier versions recorded by Little Richard and Buddy Holly, while 'Bring It On Home To Me' was one of John's "all-time favourite songs".

BONY MORONIE

This was the third song on the album retrieved from the Phil Spector sessions and probably the weakest of the batch. Lennon provides a dull, mid-tempo reading that is largely unmemorable. Again, the song had sentimental significance for the singer. "I remember singing it the only time my mother saw me perform," he explained.

YA YA

Having angered Morris Levy with a deliberately throwaway version of this song at the end of 'Walls And Bridges', Lennon makes amends with a straighter rendition which nevertheless retains the childish fun of the original.

JUST BECAUSE

The final song on offer was probably the best on the album. Lennon sets the scene, asking his listeners: "Remember this? I must have been 13 when this came out? Or was it 14? Or was it 22? I could have been 12, actually." In fact, he was 16 when Lloyd Price enjoyed his début hit with this in April 1957. Lennon later admitted that he was not that familiar with the track, which Phil Spector had strongly recommended. It works extraordinarily well as a song of emotional defiance from a former "lost weekender". Lennon instructs us to note the use of two basses on the track and towards the end of the record offers the following signing off message: "This is Dr. Winston O'Boogie saying goodnight from the Record Plant East, New York. We hope you had a swell time. Everybody here says, 'Hi'. Goodbye."

Looking back, Lennon realised that his hammy disc jockey style signing off message might have had deeper significance: "Something flashed through my mind as I said it. 'Am I really saying farewell to the business?' It wasn't conscious and it was a long, long time before I did take time out."

SHAVED FISH

RELEASED: OCTOBER 1975

[ORIGINAL UK ISSUE: APPLE PCS 7173]

The mid-Seventies saw the withdrawal of John Lennon from the record business. Soon after his reconciliation with Yoko, she became pregnant and, on the occasion of John's 35th birthday (October 9, 1975), she gave birth to Sean Tara Ono Lennon. Two weeks later, this album was issued. It was the only Lennon compilation sanctioned by the singer during his lifetime and served as an excellent opportunity to collate the A-side singles that had been issued by himself and The Plastic Ono Band since 1969. Although extremely popular, the package did not break sales records, peaking at number 8 (UK) and number 12 (US). Nevertheless, the fact that it was the only Lennon "Greatest Hits" selection of the decade ensured its continued appeal.

Detailed below are the tracks featured on the compilation that had not previously appeared on Lennon's albums.

GIVE PEACE A CHANCE

The sole crime perpetrated by this compilation was the decision to feature an agonisingly truncated version of this wonderful track, which was faded after a mere 58 seconds. Still, it partly works as a tease, reminding us of the glorious origins of The Plastic Ono Band. This remains one of the freshest and most exuberant songs ever captured on vinyl. Originally recorded on an 8-track portable recorder during their Montreal bed-in during the summer of 1969, the song featured a unique line-up of backing singers and amateur percussionists, including Yoko, Timothy Leary, Abbie Hoffman, Tommy Smothers, Murray The K, Derek Taylor, Roger Scott, several members of the clergy, a chapter of the Radha Krishna Temple and, so rumour has it, Petula Clark.

Lennon's amusing lyrics sound like a spontaneous overflowing of instant rhymes, but there is a certain sardonic glee in his litany, which embraces bagism, shagism, evolution, revolution, masturbation and much more, before leading up to the central chant, "All we are saying is give peace a chance". When the single was issued in July 1969, it was noticeable that Paul McCartney still received a writing credit, although he had nothing to do with the song. "I wasn't ready to take his name off yet," Lennon pointed out.

The song was rapidly adopted as an anthem by the peace movement and over the years took on a far greater significance. Lennon felt justly proud of the song's achievement. "I was pleased when the movement in America took up 'Give Peace A Chance'," he explained, "because I had written it with that in mind really. I hoped that instead of singing 'We Shall Overcome' from 1800 or something, they would have something contemporary. I felt an obligation, even then, to write a song that people would sing in a pub or on a demonstration."

Today, this all-purpose chant is still used by all sorts of pressure groups and is not only sung in pubs but on football terraces, where the familiar refrain "All we are saying is give us a goal" echoes through television and radio commentaries. No doubt, Lennon would have been amused.

COLD TURKEY

Unquestionably one of the most harrowing and forceful songs ever written about drug addiction, this enabled Lennon to use the primal scream to express something more than personal salvation. Set against a searing guitar backing and emphatic percussion, Lennon dramatises the disorientating effects of heroin withdrawal, feverishly pleading "I wish I was a baby/I wish I was dead". His moans and screams culminate in an intense coda during which he re-enacts the horrors of cold turkey, almost writhing in agony as he pleads, "Oh, no, no, no". It was probably the best advertisement against taking heroin ever issued, but the controversial subject matter discomfited many radio programmers in America.

"It was banned because it referred to drugs," Lennon lamented. "To me, it was a rock 'n' roll version of *The Man With The Golden Arm*. It's like banning *The Man With The Golden Arm* because it showed Frank Sinatra suffering from drug withdrawal. To ban a record is the same thing. It's like banning the movie because it shows reality."

INSTANT KARMA!

This was the ultimate example of Lennon's dream of using the 45 medium as an aural newspaper to despatch his latest message to the world. He wrote the song on the morning of January 27, 1970, and it was in the shops 10 days later. The recording, which featured a hastily assembled Plastic Ono Band line-up of George Harrison, Klaus Voormann and Alan White, was produced by Phil Spector. The tycoon of teen provided many of his wall of sound tricks from the early Sixties, using lots of echo, heavy percussion, tambourine, handclaps and multi-dubbed pianos. Lennon's passionate but controlled vocal almost bristles with static on the recording.

After working on the instrumentation and vocals at EMI, Lennon instructed his roadies to find some backing singers. The crew were directed to the Speakeasy club, where they rounded up a bunch of unsuspecting patrons who were brought back to the studio to participate in the grand chorus.

Lennon recalled the draining 12-hour session: "I wrote it in the morning on the piano, and I went into the office and I sang it many times and I sang it, and I said, 'Hell, let's do it', and we booked the studio, and Phil came in and he said: 'How do you want it?' And I said, '1950s' and he said, 'Right', and boom, I did it, in about three goes. He played it back and there it was. The only argument was I said 'a bit more bass', that's all, and off we went. Phil is great at that, he doesn't fuss about with fucking stereo or all the bullshit, just 'Does it sound all right? Then let's have it!' It doesn't matter whether something's prominent or not prominent; if it sounds good to you as a layman or as a human, take it, don't bother whether this is like that, or the quality of this... just take it, and that suits me fine."

On first hearing, the lyrics caused confusion to many listeners as the word "karma" was not in such general use at the time among the general public. In Lennon's circle, of course, "karma" was slowly on its way to cliché status. "Everybody was going on about karma, especially in the Sixties," he opined, a decade on. "But it occurred to me that karma is instant as well, as it influences your past life or your future life. There really is a reaction to what you do now. That's what people ought to be concerned about. Also, I'm fascinated by commercials and promotion as an art form. I enjoy them. So the idea of instant karma was like the idea of instant coffee, presenting something in a new form."

For those unsure about karma, the song offered various meanings. Some latched on to the concept of receiving enlightenment like instant coffee, while others saw a left-wing political or even Christian message in the line, "Better recognise your brother, everyone you meet". There was even a hint of tart Lennon sarcasm in the lines, "Who do you think you are, a superstar? Well, right you are".

In a determined attempt to bring his message to the masses, Lennon premièred the song on BBC's *Top Of The Pops* on February 11, 1970, the first time he had appeared on the show since the heyday of The Beatles. It was a remarkable visual performance from The Plastic Ono Band, with rarely seen Beatles' roadie Mal Evans playing tambourine, and Yoko sitting, wearing a blindfold, holding up peace cards and, most strikingly, knitting.

POWER TO THE PEOPLE

Another instant slogan from Lennon, this time for his far left friends. The indecision once present on The Beatles' 'Revolution' ("count me out... count me in") is replaced by cast iron conviction as he enthuses: "Say you want a revolution?/We better get it on right away".

Musically, it's a catchy, anthemic piece, buoyed by a gospel chorus and the fierce, rasping saxophone of Bobby Keys. In interviews, the song enabled Lennon to spout his socialist ideals. "They knock me for saying 'Power To The People' and say that no one section should have the power," he complained. "Rubbish! The people aren't a section. The people means everyone. I think that everyone should own everything equally and that the people should own part of the factories and they should have some say in who is the boss and who does what. Students should be able to select teachers. It might be like communism, but I don't really know what real communism is."

Like several of Lennon's later political songs, 'Power To The People' offered a slogan rather than a solution. There was at least an awareness of women's issues hidden away in the verses as Lennon advised: "I gotta ask you comrade and brother/How do you treat your own woman back home?/She got to be herself..." But, amid the over the top Spector production, it was the song's title alone that blared from radio sets and phonograms: "Power to the people, right on!"

Looking back from the more jaundiced perspective of 1980, Lennon remarked: "I remember that was the expression going round those days... Tariq Ali had kept coming round wanting money for the *Red Mole* or some magazine... I used to give anybody money, kind of out of guilt... I was thinking, 'Well, I'm working class and I am not one of them, but I am rich so therefore I have to'. So any time anybody said something like that I would fork out... I kind of wrote 'Power To The People' in a way kind of as a guilt song... It's like a newspaper song – when you write about something instant that's going on right now. I don't call it a well-crafted song or anything, just that was the news headline with misprints and everything. But the B-side was 'Open Your Box', which is worth a play."

HAPPY XMAS (WAR IS OVER)

One of the greatest Christmas songs ever written, this song began life as a poster campaign. In December 1969, the Lennons bought billboard space in 12 cities, including London, New York, Hollywood, Toronto, Berlin, Paris, Rome, Tokyo and Athens. Their message proclaimed: "War Is Over! If You Want It. Happy Christmas From John & Yoko". Almost two years on, the duo decided to record a seasonal single, using the slogan as their theme. It was a remarkable record in many ways, not least because it allowed Phil Spector to show off the same production talents that had graced his 1963 festive celebration 'A Christmas Gift To You'. With the Lennons, he provided the familiar sleigh bells and tight harmonies, even recruiting the Harlem Community Choir to spectacular effect. John showed himself as a master of ambiguity with the arresting opening line to the song, which seemed both reflective and accusative: "And so this is

Christmas/And what have you done?"

The only regrettable feature of the record was its timing. "As usual, we messed it up," Lennon admitted. "We recorded it a bit too late. We almost missed the Christmas market that year." This was no exaggeration. Amazingly, the single failed to enter the US Top 40, which was a terrible injustice. Equally disappointing was its delayed release in the UK due to the dispute over Yoko's writing credit. It finally appeared in Britain one year later in December 1972 and was a regular chart contender for many years thereafter. Lennon was proud of its longevity. As he explained to the BBC's Andy Peebles: "What we wanted to do was have something besides 'White Christmas' being played every Christmas. And there's always wars, right; there's always somebody getting shot. So, every year you could play it and there's always somebody being tortured or shot somewhere. So the lyric stands in that respect... I've always wanted to write something that would be a Christmas record, that would last forever."

GIVE PEACE A CHANCE REPRISE

The compilation ends with 'Happy Xmas (War Is Over)' segueing into this 50-second live version of 'Give Peace A Chance' taken from the August 1972 One To One concert. *Newsweek* magazine neatly summed up the impact of the song: "It will serve as the centrepiece for sing-ins at shopping centres planned in Washington and will join the list of carols to be sung in projected nation-wide Christmas Eve demonstrations... The peace movement has found an anthem."

Full Track Listing: 'Give Peace A Chance'; 'Cold Turkey'; 'Instant Karma!'; 'Power To The People'; 'Mother'; 'Woman Is The Nigger Of The World'; 'Imagine'; 'Whatever Gets You Thru The Night'; 'Mind Games'; '#9 Dream'; (a) 'Happy Xmas (War Is Over)' (b) 'Give Peace A Chance': 'Reprise'.

John Lennon   Double Fantasy   Yoko Ono

DOUBLE FANTASY

RELEASED: NOVEMBER 1980

[ORIGINAL UK ISSUE: GEFFEN K 99131]

Following the birth of his son Sean, John Lennon elected to become a house husband, fulfilling the fatherly obligations that had been so patently lacking in the rearing of his first boy Julian. The self-imposed decision meant that he could finally break the cycle of abandonment that had begun in his own disrupted childhood, when his parents had given him no time instead of it all. Although Lennon's retreat to domesticity was later seen as a fully-fledged retirement, he had always intended to return to his musical career once Sean had reached five years of age.

For the remainder of the Seventies, he kept to his word and never once entered a recording studio or appeared on a stage. His only concession to the creative urge was to tinker with some home demos, usually just after his birthday each year. It was not until 1980 that he seriously began working on a new album, which soon developed into a musical dialogue between himself and Yoko. With Jack Douglas installed as co-producer and the newly formed Geffen Records signing the Lennons, the work was completed in a flurry of recording sessions in preparation for a pre-Christmas release.

When 'Double Fantasy' finally appeared, critical reaction was sharply divided. British reviewers, still caught up in the maelstrom of post punk, felt disappointed by its flaccidity and found it cloying in comparison to his previous work. They were hoping for something in the spirit of 'Cold Turkey' and found only cosy sentimentality. American critics were generally more generous, and even the radical Robert Christgau of *Village Voice* wrote an eloquent appraisal, testifying to Lennon's new maturity.

In his last ever interview, conducted with RKO Radio on 8 December 1980,

Lennon expressed his own feelings about the album's significance: "When I was writing this, I was visualising all the people of my age group for the Sixties being in their thirties and forties now, just like me, and having wives and children and having gone through everything together. I'm singing for them... I'm saying, 'Here I am now. How are you? How's your relationship going? Did you get through it all? Wasn't the Seventies a drag, you know? Here we are. Well, let's try to make the Eighties good, you know, because it's still up to us to make what we can of it'... We were the hip ones in the Sixties, but the world is not like the Sixties. The whole world's changed and we're going into an unknown future, but we're still all here."

Albums released by major artistes after long absences always prompt high expectations and 'Double Fantasy' was no exception. Despite many critics' reservations, it clearly contained some of Lennon's best work, and some pretty average material too. Perhaps the most surprising aspect of the album was the emergence of Yoko Ono as a convincingly commercial writer, with a couple of harder-edged songs that had a punch missing from her husband's more contented meditations. While the overall feel of the album suggested middle-aged satisfaction, a closer listen to several of the tracks indicated some conflict amid the Edenic bliss. The production gloss sometimes disguised the starker moments on the record, but they were there, dramatised within the "answer song" format. As Lennon said: "The work we did on this is really a play, but we used ourselves as characters".

For most listeners, it was just good to hear Lennon singing again after such a long hiatus. In interviews, he spoke of touring the record in the New Year and promised that a follow-up, already apparently underway, would be completed soon. Given his restless spirit, it is not easy to predict what Lennon might have done next, especially considering the contemporaneous work of Yoko Ono, whose intriguing 'Walking On Thin Ice' he was producing during the final days of his life. He spoke of "a new era of

Lennon/Ono music", which presumably embraced the ongoing romantic saga of John and Yoko in the form of a sequel to 'Double Fantasy', plus the more radical experimentation that he had enjoyed since the controversial days of 'Two Virgins'. No doubt, Lennon and Ono would have continued to release work, together and apart. Whatever might have been achieved was lost in the madness that prompted a deranged Beatles' fan to murder his tainted idol. The dream was over.

(JUST LIKE) STARTING OVER

The album opens with the sound of Yoko's wishing bell, its gentle tinkling deliberately intended to remind the listener of the contrasting funereal bells of 'Mother', the first track on Lennon's premier solo work. Whereas 'Mother' had revealed Lennon in the throes of intense pain, 'Starting Over' was an optimistic reiteration of love's vows, and looked towards a happy middle age. Its lyrics were completed during the summer of 1980.

As Lennon explained: "I wrote it when I was in Bermuda with Sean, while Yoko was attending to business. It just came out that way. All the other songs were finished and it and 'Cleanup Time' came out sort of like fun after the work was done. It has the Fiftiesish sound because I have never really written a song that sounded like that period, although that was my period, the music I identified with. So I just thought, 'Why the hell not?' In the Beatle days that would have been taken as a joke. One avoided clichés. But, of course, now those clichés are not clichés anymore. I nearly took out the words 'spread our wings and fly' because I thought, 'Oh God, they'll all be saying: "What's that about Wings?"' It has nothing to do with Wings!"

Musically, the song was quite simple, with Lennon attempting to undercut the schmaltzy arrangement and sentimental lyrics with an opening mock rockabilly vocal. Although it was not the best song on the album, its theme of renewal could be interpreted as an advert for the Lennons' comeback and so served as an obvious pilot single. According to John, the song's title was slightly amended at the eleventh hour: "It was really called 'Starting Over' but, while we're making it, people kept putting things out with the same title. There was a country 'n' western hit called 'Starting Over', so I added '(Just Like)' at the last minute... The musicians got very loose because it was so simple rock 'n' roll... 'Starting Over' was the best way to start over. And, to me, it was like going back to 15 and singing *à la* Presley... I was referring to 'Elvis Orbison'. It's kind of 'I Want You, I Need You...', 'Only The Lonely'... a kind of parody, but not really parody."

KISS KISS KISS

This track offered proof of Yoko's commercial and contemporary sound, with Andy Newark's drums prominent in the mix and the vocal surprisingly pleasant and in tune. In earlier years she might have screamed her lungs out for 10 minutes, but here she offers a brief and erotically charged orgasmic moan to bring

the song to a startling conclusion. Her faked climax both astounded and amused those present.

"I started to do it," she told the BBC, "and then I suddenly looked and all these engineers were all looking and I thought, 'I can't do that'. So I said, 'Turn off all the lights'... They put the screen around me and I did it that way."

CLEANUP TIME

"It's a piano lick, with words added," Lennon explained, when recalling the origin of this satisfied tale of domestic union. "I was talking to [co-producer] Jack Douglas on the phone from Bermuda," he continued. "We were talking about the Seventies and about people's getting out of drugs and alcohol and those kind of things. And he said, 'Well, it's clean-up time, right?' And I said, 'It sure is'. That was the end of the conversation. I went straight to the piano and just started boogieing and 'Cleanup Time' came out. Then I had the music and thought, 'What is this about?' I only had the title. So then I wrote the story on top of the music. It's sort of a description of John and Yoko in their palace, the Palace of Versailles, the Dakota: 'The queen is in the counting house, counting up the money; the king is in the kitchen...' "

GIVE ME SOMETHING

An acid answer to 'Cleanup Time', and far more impressive, this chilling and accusative song features Ono tearing down the John and Yoko myth of domestic bliss. It sets a pattern for much of the album with John romanticising their relationship while Yoko takes a more cynical view of proceedings. At the end of the song, she even adopts a self-martyred tone: "And I'll give you my heartbeat/And a bit of tear and flesh/It's not very much but while it's there/You can have it, you can have it".

I'M LOSING YOU

Lennon returned to the more familiar lyrical territory of emotional insecurity for this track, which emerged as one of the best on the album. Its pent up anger and fear of losing Yoko propels John back to earlier memories of their last estrangement. Indeed, one verse in the song reads like an outtake from the lost weekend: "I know I hurt you then/But hell that was way back when/And well, do you still have to carry that cross?/Don't want to hear about it".

Lennon confirmed that the song spanned two eras of emotional disturbance: "It's a song about the past, but I actually started writing it when I called from Bermuda and I couldn't get through to Yoko. I was just mad as hell, feeling lost and separate. But it's also a description of the separation period in the early Seventies when I physically couldn't get through."

He later added, "But, getting a bit distant from it, it is expressing the losing you, of the 18 months lost... losing one's mother, losing one's everything, losing everything you've ever lost in that song..."

I'M MOVING ON

'I'm Losing You' dramatically segues into Yoko Ono's answer song, which is her best moment on the album. The lyrics actually date back to 1973, when their relationship was clearly in trouble, but the idea of reviving the song as a spiteful riposte was truly inspired. In a remarkable diatribe, Yoko accuses Lennon of fickleness, infidelity and, worst of all perhaps, being a phoney. The song provides a welcome moment of harsh realism, which splendidly undercuts the sometimes cloying depiction of John and Yoko's fairy-tale marriage.

BEAUTIFUL BOY (DARLING BOY)

Although some would see this song as over-sentimental, it was still a fine example of Lennon's rejection of traditional macho rock ideals. His description of the father/son relationship is very poignant in places and there is even a nice touch of homespun philosophy in the line, "Life is

what happens to you while you're busy making other plans".

The ballad was apparently in the back of Lennon's mind for some time before he completed a home demo of the song in late 1979. As he explained: "I was with Sean in the kitchen with the bread... I kept thinking, 'Well, I ought to be inspired to write about Sean'... I was going through a bit of that and when I finally gave up on thinking about writing a song about him, of course, the song came to me."

In common with several other songs on the album, the lyrics took on a sadly ironic ring in view of his impending death. Almost in passing, he sings, "I can hardly wait/To see you come of age/But I guess we'll both /Just have to be patient". These were the words of a man who felt he still had all the time in the world.

WATCHING THE WHEELS

Another of Lennon's great tracks, this was his provocative defence of indolence, a theme previously heard to strong effect on The Beatles' 'I'm Only

Sleeping'. The inspiration for the song came from reading other people's comments on his extended sabbatical from the music business. "Pop stars were getting indignant in the press that I wasn't making records," he laughed. "I couldn't believe it. They were acting like mothers-in-law. I don't know whether it was Mick [Jagger] or who. What's it got to do with them if I never do another record in my life?"

His rejection of the music business rat race was almost as radical a statement as 'Give Peace A Chance' or 'Woman Is The Nigger Of The World'. He often recalled the surprise he felt in realising that life did not stop when his name no longer appeared in the music trade magazine *Billboard*. "I just had to let it go," he could say, with satisfaction.

The image of the wheel in the song's title also allowed Lennon to indulge in some quasi-mystical speculation during interviews. "The whole universe is a wheel, right?" he imparted sagely to *Rolling Stone*. "Wheels go round and round. They're my own wheels mainly. Watching meself is like watching every-body else. And I watch myself through my child too... The hardest part is facing yourself. It's easier to shout about 'Revolution' and 'Power To The People' than it is to look at yourself and try to find out what's real inside you and what isn't..."

I'M YOUR ANGEL

Between the fade-out of 'Watching The Wheels' and the beginning of this track, there is a brief segue of music and recorded conversation. Journalist Jonathan Cott was sufficiently intrigued by the effect to tease the following lengthy explanation from Lennon: "One of the voices is me going, 'God bless you, man, thank you, you've got a lucky face', which is what the English guys who beg or want a tip say, so that's what you hear me mumbling. And then we re-created the sounds of what Yoko and I call the Strawberries and Violin room – the Palm Court at the Plaza Hotel. We like to sit there occasionally and listen to the old violin and have a cup of tea and some strawberries. It's romantic. And so the picture is: There's this kind of street prophet, Hyde Park Corner-type guy who just watches the wheels going around, pronouncing on whatever he's pronouncing on. And people are throwing money in his hat, and he's saying, 'Thank you, thank you'. And then you get in the horse carriage and you go around New York and go into the hotel and the violins are playing and then this woman comes and sings about being an angel."

Alas, the actual song proves terribly anti-climactic, with Yoko reverting to her baby voice, set against a Twenties style arrangement. The melody so closely resembled that of the evergreen 'Making Whoopee' that the publishers subsequently sought damages for alleged plagiarism.

WOMAN

This song featured the most beautiful melody on the album and it was no surprise when it climbed to number 1 in the UK charts following Lennon's murder. On one level, the composition can be seen as an obsequious tribute to Yoko, but

Lennon felt that it held a more universal message. "That's to Yoko and to all women in a way," he told *Playboy*'s David Sheff. "My history of relationships with women is a very poor one – very macho, very stupid, very typical of a certain type of man, I suppose, which is very sensitive and insecure but acting aggressive and macho. You know, trying to cover up the feminine side, which I still have a tendency to do. But I'm learning to acknowledge that it's all right to be soft because that side of me is the comfortable side of me. It's like I tend to put my cowboy boots on when I'm insecure, whereas now I'm in sneakers and it's comfy."

While some commentators saw the song simply as a mainstream ballad, those familiar with Lennon's *oeuvre* took a wider view of its significance. Tracing a history of Lennon's love songs and comments on women, it is possible to see a gradual development from the macho cool narrator of 'Girl', through the proselytising new man campaigner in 'Woman Is The Nigger Of The World' to the humble house husband of 'Woman'.

Lennon was equally keen to place 'Woman' in some kind of historical context. When interviewed by the BBC, he suggested: "It sounds a bit like 'Girl' and a bit Beatley, but I do like it... I'm supposed to be macho, Butch Cassidy or something and tough Lennon with the leather jacket and swearing. And I really am just as romantic as the next guy, and I always was. It's sort of an Eighties version of 'Girl' to me. I call this one the Beatle track... It suddenly sort of hit me about what women represent to us, not as the sex object or the mother, but just their contribution. That's why you hear me muttering at the beginning 'For the other half of the sky', which is Chairman Mao's famous statement. That it is the other half. All this thing about man, woman, man woman, is a joke. Without each other, there ain't nothing... It was a different viewpoint of what I'd felt about woman and I can't express it better than I said in the song."

BEAUTIFUL BOYS

Yoko extends the thematic framework of Lennon's 'Beautiful Boy' to comment on both her son and husband. Addressing each in turn, she includes an interesting observation on John's psychology: "You got all you can carry/And still feel somehow empty". The song encourages exploration ("Don't be afraid to go to hell and back"), but concludes with the gentle warning, "Don't be afraid to be afraid". While mulling over that line, Lennon added: "I'm not afraid to be afraid, though it's always scary. But it's more painful to try not to be yourself. People spend a lot of time trying to be somebody else."

DEAR YOKO

If '(Just Like) Starting Over' was Lennon's vocal tribute to Elvis Presley and Roy Orbison, then this was an even more obvious homage to Buddy Holly. It is also 'Oh Yoko' revisited, with Lennon again expressing affection for his wife by cataloguing her ever present influence upon the most mundane aspects of his daily life. While other writers might have fictionalised the experience or referred more obliquely to an unnamed muse, Lennon clearly preferred to be as particular and direct as possible. As he noted: "The track's a nice track and it happens to be about my wife instead of 'Dear Sandra' or some other person that a singer would sing about who may or may not exist."

EVERY MAN HAS A WOMAN WHO LOVES HIM

One of the less melodic songs on the album with a generally unexciting arrangement, this track featured Yoko musing over the contradictory elements of her relationship with Lennon. There is also a strong suggestion of her own fickleness: "Why do I roam when I know you're the one/Why do I run when I feel like holding you".

HARD TIMES ARE OVER

Yoko is allowed the last word with this anthemic finale, which offers the comforts of middle-aged security after a lifetime of struggle. The chorus includes a crucial qualification: "hard times are over *for a while*"). Soon, it would be clear how short those good times were to be.

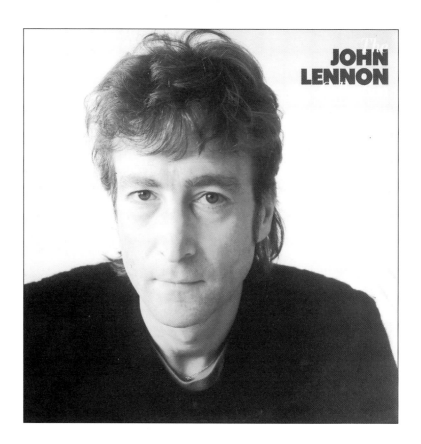

The
JOHN
LENNON

THE JOHN LENNON COLLECTION

RELEASED: NOVEMBER 1982

[ORIGINAL UK ISSUE: PARLOPHONE EMTV 37]

With strong promotion on television in the UK, this compilation climbed to number 1, in striking contrast to its disappointing performance in the US charts, where it stalled at number 33. Reasonably generous, with 19 tracks on the CD version, ('Move Over Ms L' and 'Cold Turkey' are missing from the vinyl release), the collection inevitably concentrated on Lennon's more commercial material. The fact that it featured only one track from 'John Lennon/Plastic Ono Band', placed quietly out of the way near the end of Side one, speaks volumes. However, it did offer the first appearance of the original single 'Give Peace A Chance' on album, although the inner sleeve erroneously states "From the EMI album 'Shaved Fish'," apparently unaware that the previous compilation had only offered the first 58 seconds of the song.

GIVE PEACE A CHANCE

The album was worth the retail price for the chance to hear the full version of this song on CD for the first time. It remains as fresh and exuberant as ever and the perfect example of Lennon's desire to make The Plastic Ono Band a sort of people's collective. Recalling the recording for the BBC, he explained: "There was Tommy Smothers and Tim Leary and Dick Gregory and all people sort of clapping along and singing on the chorus. And if you hear the record, it's funny actually, because my rhythm sense has always been a bit wild and, half-way through it, I got on the on-beat instead of the back beat and it was hard because there was non-musicians playing along with us. So I had to put a lot of tape echo to double up the beat to keep a steady beat right through the whole record..."

Actually, Lennon did a bit more than that, adding percussion from Ringo Starr back in the recording studio and overdubbing a full choir of session singers. In order to ensure that the record did not receive a radio ban, Lennon subtly altered the lyric sheet to remove a potentially offensive word. "I sort of cheated," he admitted. "I'd had enough of bannings and all... I'd been banned so many times all over that I copped out and wrote 'mastication'." In the lyric sheet to this collection, the self-censorship is overridden and the third verse now features the line: "Revolution, evolution, *masturbation*...."

Full track listing: 'Give Peace A Chance'; 'Instant Karma!'; 'Power To The People'; 'Whatever Gets You Thru The Night'; '# 9 Dream'; 'Mind Games'; 'Love'; 'Happy Xmas (War Is Over)'; 'Imagine'; 'Jealous Guy'; 'Stand By Me'; '(Just Like) Starting Over'; 'Woman'; 'I'm Losing You'; 'Beautiful Boy (Darling Boy)'; 'Watching The Wheels'; 'Dear Yoko'; 'Move Over Ms L'; 'Cold Turkey'.

MOVE OVER MS L

The CD release of the album featured this surprise bonus track, which had previously been available only on the B-side of the single 'Stand By Me'. Written during the famous "lost weekend" exile, it's a sardonic and irreverent riposte by John to his estranged wife. Musically, it borrows heavily from Chuck Berry's 'Roll Over Beethoven'.

John Lennon

HEART PLAY
—unfinished dialogue—

Yoko Ono

HEART PLAY –
AN UNFINISHED DIALOGUE

RELEASED: DECEMBER 1983

[ORIGINAL UK ISSUE: POLYDOR 817 238-1]

This interview disc consisted of chunks of conversation with the Lennons during the promotion of 'Double Fantasy'. It is dominated by choice extracts from the *Playboy* interview which are spoiled only by the interviewer's acquiescent tone and nervous habit of saying "a-ha" every few seconds. In fact, it's more of a monologue than a conversation, with Lennon in sparkling form throughout. He reveals that 'Double Fantasy' is the first of a two-volume work and hopes that the world is at last ready to accept Yoko as his equal musical partner. At one point he credits her for refusing "to live with a bullshit artist, which I'm pretty good at".

At times, it's poignant and painful listening, as Lennon marvels at the old adage "life begins at 40" and expresses great excitement for the future. His current album is described as the product of "love and a lot of sweat and life's experiences of two people".

On the second side of the record, he reflects on The Beatles' break-up and cuts through the myths and nostalgia with his usual forthrightness. Denying his guru role for the umpteenth time, he tells his audience, "I can't cure you – you cure you". The album ends on an eerie note, with Lennon discussing the world's great peace campaigners and adding, with prophetic poignancy: "What does it mean when you're a pacifist that you get shot. I can never understand that".

John Lennon Milk and Honey Yoko Ono

MILK AND HONEY: A HEART PLAY

RELEASED: JANUARY 1984

[ORIGINAL UK ISSUE: POLYDOR POLH 5]

Released shortly after the third anniversary of Lennon's death, this was seen by some as tantamount to the follow-up to 'Double Fantasy'. The assumption was that the Lennon songs were outtakes intended for an album already named as 'Milk And Honey'. Tracing back the origins of the songs, however, it is clear that what we have here are demos that were recorded at the very beginning of the 'Double Fantasy' sessions and subsequently discarded. Some of the tracks are so impressive that it is difficult to believe that Lennon wouldn't have unearthed and revamped them at a later date. Then again, he might have gone ahead and recorded a completely new set of songs and never returned to these. At the time of these recordings, Lennon had summed up their potential with the quip: "I'm going back to my roots. It's like Dylan doing 'Nashville Skyline'".

The second misconception surrounding this album was that the Yoko tracks were also 'Double Fantasy' outtakes. It has since emerged that, with the exception of 'Let Me Count The Ways', all this material was recorded after John's death.

Despite the piecemeal way it was put together and the different time scale of the recordings, the whole works far better than might have been expected. Some of Yoko's songs cry out for the quality control that John might have pro- vided, but most of his previously rejected stuff sounds startlingly good. Many of the critics who lampooned 'Double Fantasy' openly stated that it would have been a much better and more sprightly album if Lennon had only included a couple of the rough hewed tracks present on this set.

Since this album, Yoko Ono has been sparing in providing further session tapes, although she did pass on two tracks, 'Free As A Bird' and 'Real Love', to the remaining Beatles. However, there remains on tape a number of unreleased songs in various stages of development, including such titles as 'Mirror Mirror On The Wall', 'She Is A Friend Of Dorothy's', 'One Of The Boys', 'My Life', 'I'm Crazy', 'Serve Yourself', 'The Worst Is Over', 'Life Begins At 40', 'You Saved My Soul' and 'Dear John'. Other rarities have also been aired on the Westwood One US radio series *The Lost Lennon Tapes*. It seems likely that another archive work, most likely a box set, will feature this material at some time in the distant future.

I'M STEPPING OUT

"1-2-3-4", Lennon begins in classic rock 'n' roll fashion, as he narrates the following autobiography: "This here's the story about a house husband who, you know, just has to get out of the house. He's been looking at the kids for days and days, he's been washing the dishes and screwing around... until he's going crazy".

What follows is a refreshingly upbeat opener, in striking contrast to much of the

more polished material on 'Double Fantasy'. The rawness of the rehearsal fits Lennon's bristling statement of independence: "If it don't feel right, don't do it/Just leave a message on the phone and tell them to screw it". What most impresses is Lennon's irrepressible excitement at the prospect of simply going out into the street. Like a cured agoraphobic, he can barely suppress his joy at the prospect of stepping out.

SLEEPLESS NIGHT

Yoko reinforces her voice with lots of echo as she relates this humorous tale of a sleepless night. There's a basic rock 'n' roll beat, with some playful phrasing from Ono, as she quizzically wonders, "What am I asking for?"

I DON'T WANNA FACE IT

Another exuberant rocker from Lennon with basic lyrics and all the spirit of an early rehearsal. Musically, the song reveals his long-standing debt to Fifties' rock 'n' roll. There is an endearing lack of self-consciousness about the track, with Lennon content to keep things simple. It is worth contrasting the sentiments of this song with those of 'I'm Stepping Out'.

DON'T BE SCARED

Yoko offers a series of quaint but simple aphorisms set against an insistent reggae beat. Whether Lennon would have deemed this track worthy of album release without substantial development seems doubtful.

NOBODY TOLD ME

Issued as a single just before the album's release, this track proved a revelation to many critics and fans. It provoked several commentators to suggest that 'Double Fantasy' would have been considerably better if only Lennon had approached that album in the same spirit as this song. In many respects, it's Lennon at his spontaneous best, using a catchy melody and getting a quick take with piano, guitar and drums. The sound is upfront, in the spirit of The Plastic Ono Band, the lyrics are witty and unselfconscious, and Lennon's vocal is at its biting best. It should have been a number 1 hit.

O SANITY

The first side of the album ends with this short, simple melody from Yoko, which proves surprisingly effective. She includes the usual lyrical aphorisms, but also addresses 'sanity' as though it were a recalcitrant child: "O sanity, o sanity, why don't you let me go/Let me go, cut it out!"

BORROWED TIME

Another posthumous single, this Caribbean flavoured track, complete with simulated steel drum, was another of Lennon's testimonies to the virtues of growing old. There's a comic monologue and some playful singing towards the end of the song, but in the aftermath of his death such lines as "Living on borrowed time/Without a thought for tomorrow" have been invested with a painful poignancy.

YOUR HANDS

Yoko sings in Japanese and translates accordingly. The backing is fairly rudimentary as she once again revisits the theme of John and Yoko's insatiable love.

(FORGIVE ME) MY LITTLE FLOWER PRINCESS

There's some debate as to whether Lennon was inspired to write this track for May Pang or Yoko Ono, although the lyrical evidence points firmly towards the latter. It's Lennon at his most deferential and submissive, singing an early take that would, most likely, have been changed substantially if released in his lifetime.

LET ME COUNT THE WAYS

This would appear to be the one Yoko song on the album which was recorded, however primitively, during Lennon's lifetime. Taken from a standard cassette recording, this basic tune on piano testifies to a composition that might have been impressive, if developed. The lyrics are expansive and

completely unlike Yoko's usual instant haikus, a discrepancy explained by the fact that the source of the song is the 19th century poet, Elizabeth Barrett Browning. Yoko explained the genesis of the composition: "One early morning in the summer of 1980, I woke up with 'Let Me Count The Ways' ringing in my head. I called John who was then in Bermuda and played it over the phone. 'How do you like it?' 'I really like it. It's beautiful'. 'How about you writing one with a Robert Browning line and we'll have portraits of us as Elizabeth and Robert on the cover?' (This needs a little explaining. John and I always thought, among many other things, that we were maybe the reincarnation of Robert and Liz. So he immediately knew what I was talking about.) We discussed then about [the] 'Double Fantasy' cover, that it should be two portraits, one of Elizabeth and the other of Robert, only the faces would be ours. John thought we should look very prim and proper with just our hands coming out of the paintings and holding in the middle, the funny touch. We both laughed. 'OK then, just tell downstairs (our office) to send me the collection of Robert Browning and let's see what happens'. It wasn't necessary, however, to send the collection to Bermuda. John called me that afternoon. 'Hey, you won't believe this!' He explained that he was watching the TV, a Fifties film of a baseball player. In the film, John saw the girlfriend send a poem which was one by Robert Browning called 'Grow Old Beside Me'. 'Can you believe that?... so, anyway, this is my version'. John proudly played his song over the phone. That's how our two songs happened."

GROW OLD WITH ME

John's answer song to Yoko's 'Let Me Count The Ways' survives in this rough, home-made cassette version in which he plays piano and sings falsetto. Melodically, it's not unlike 'Woman', with romantic lyrics that again proclaim the joys of love in old age. According to Yoko: "To us, these two songs were the backbone of 'Double Fantasy', and we kept discussing how we would arrange them. For John, 'Grow Old With Me' was one that would be a standard, the kind that they would play in church every time a couple gets married. It was horns and symphony time. But we were working against deadline for the Christmas release of the album, [so we] kept holding 'Grow Old With Me' to the end, and finally decided it was better to leave the song for 'Milk And Honey'... 'Grow Old With Me' was a song John made several cassettes of, as we discussed the arrangements for it. Everybody around us knew how important these cassettes were. They were in safe-keeping, some in our bedroom, some in our cassette file, and some in a vault. All of them disappeared since then, except the one on this record. It may be that it was meant to be this way, since the version that was left to us was John's last recording. The one John and I recorded together in our bedroom with a piano and a rhythm box."

YOU'RE THE ONE

Yoko closes the album with the sound of a thunderstorm as she backs herself with rhythmic yelps and lyrics that are as sparse and elliptical as anything she ever wrote.

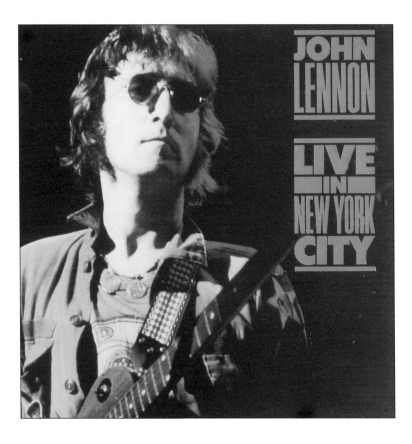

LIVE IN NEW YORK CITY

RELEASED: FEBRUARY 1986

[ORIGINAL UK ISSUE: PARLOPHONE PCS 7301]

The famous One To One concert had been bootlegged over the years but this was its first official appearance, nearly 14 years after the original performance. Yoko Ono remixed the record and receives the production credit on the album. Commenting on the memorable recording, she explained: "The concert was held in Madison Square Garden, August 30, 1972, to help improve the living conditions of the mentally handicapped children. Starting with the Toronto Peace Festival in 1969, John and I did a series of rock concerts as our statement of Peace and Love, and to spotlight various social issues effectively. All proceeds from the concerts were given to the needy. This one in Madison Square Garden turned out to be the last concert John and I did together."

As an archive live recording, it's a welcome addition to the Lennon canon, enabling us to hear several classic studio songs in a concert setting.

NEW YORK CITY

A chant of 'Power To The People' opens the concert before Lennon launches into a stirring version of 'New York City', with the grandly named Plastic Ono Elephant's Memory Band providing a suitably rudimentary backing. The vocals are mixed surprisingly low in places, which robs the song of some of its power.

IT'S SO HARD

Continuing with a basic blues riff, Lennon tackles one of the harder-edged songs on 'Imagine', while saxophonist Stan Bronstein is given leave to let rip. Lennon slows the pace so that his singing is virtually reduced to a spoken word recitation in places. "Welcome to the rehearsal," he chirps at the end of the number.

WOMAN IS THE NIGGER OF THE WORLD

With Yoko's 'We're All Water' edited from the original tape, we move straight into the Lennons' most famous feminist statement. Although the vocal is a little flat in places, the performance transcends such minor quibbles, providing us with a welcome opportunity to hear a live version of one of the best Lennon songs of the decade.

WELL WELL WELL

'Sisters O Sisters' was the next song at the concert, but Yoko edits her version, moving swiftly on to another blues based item. Somebody shouts for Ringo just before the song starts, prompting Lennon to retort, "That was yesterday, or four years ago". Although this track was far from the best song on 'John Lennon/Plastic Ono Band', it works remarkably well in live performance and Lennon even attempts some screaming at the end, albeit in less tortured fashion than on the studio version.

INSTANT KARMA! (WE ALL SHINE ON)

"I'm only beginning to understand what this record was about," Lennon remarks, as they attempt a relatively sparse version of 'Instant Karma!' Without Phil Spector's studio magic, the song sounds strangely denuded and even the presence of two drummers, Jim Keltner and Rick Frank, cannot quite produce a sound to equal the percussive power of the original. A better mixed version might have brought up the drums in the appropriate places. By the end, the song is turned into a chant, after which Lennon apologises: "We'll get it right next time".

MOTHER

"This song is another song from one of those albums I made since I left The Rolling Stones," Lennon jokes. "And a lot of people thought it was *just* about my parents, but it's about 99 per cent of the parents alive, or half-dead." Again, it's most gratifying to hear one of Lennon's finest songs in live performance and this version is particularly striking. With a strong saxophone backing, Lennon turns the song into a blues, bringing out much of the pain in lines like "I needed you so bad, you didn't need me, oh no!" Towards the end, he attempts the primal scream, investing as much passion in his voice as possible, albeit with the knowledge that he cannot risk shouting himself hoarse for fear of destroying the rest of the show.

COME TOGETHER

"We'll go back in the past just once," Lennon concedes. "You might remember this better than I do, actually. Something about a flat top, that's all I know." The song must have been on his mind at the time, as music publisher Morris Levy was suing him for alleged plagiarism of Chuck Berry's 'You Can't Catch Me'. Lennon provides a potent performance and Elephant's Memory find an impressive R&B groove. As the song ends, Lennon proudly says: "Thank you, I nearly got all the words right too."

IMAGINE

"This song's more about why we're here, apart from rocking and all that," Lennon notes. Both his vocal and piano playing are tentative here, but he relates the song to the audience, amending the lyrics a little to say "Imagine no possessions, I wonder if *we* can" and expressing his feminist leanings by suggesting "a brotherhood and sisterhood of man".

COLD TURKEY

"This is something that happens to us, one way or another," Lennon stresses as he re-enters the harrowing memories of heroin withdrawal. The song is taken at a surprisingly fast pace and some of the menace of the original recording is lost due to the chug-a-long accompaniment. Towards the end, though, Lennon unearths the buried pain with some expressive vocal outpourings.

HOUND DOG

Recalling Elvis Presley's version of 'Hound Dog', Lennon observed that it often sounded as though it was being played at a different speed, depending on his mood of the moment. "One day it would sound very slow," he considered, "and one day it would sound very fast. It was just my feeling towards it... the way I heard it." It is perhaps surprising then, that he plays the song in exactly the same tempo as the original. It's a great finale, complemented by a thrilling sax break and some excellent boogie woogie piano.

GIVE PEACE A CHANCE

"This is what you call an encore," Lennon announces. "You're going to be the encore too!" At that point, the audience really does become The Plastic Ono Band. As Yoko recalled: "The concert was filled with love of brotherhood and sisterhood. We passed out tambourines to the audience, true to our slogan, 'You are The Plastic Ono Band'. Everybody joined in on stage at the end when we sang 'Give Peace A Chance'. People could not contain themselves and marched down Fifth Avenue after the performance, singing 'Give Peace A Chance'." It is a pity that the album could not include more than a few seconds of this atmospheric conclusion, which went on for 10 minutes and featured Stevie Wonder's vocal accompaniment.

John Lennón: 1940-1980
The Song Is Over

JOHN LENNON   MENLOVE AVE

MENLOVE AVENUE

RELEASED: OCTOBER 1986

[ORIGINAL UK ISSUE: PARLOPHONE PCS 7308]

Shortly after what would have been Lennon's 46th birthday, Yoko Ono sanctioned this archive release, which offered a side of outtakes from 'Rock 'n' Roll' and a side of rehearsal sessions from 'Walls And Bridges'. The packaging was slight, but the cover featured an illustration of Lennon drawn by Andy Warhol. Overall, it was a welcome release for collectors and hard-core fans, and provided insights into the making of both albums. The 'Rock 'n' Roll' outtakes offer the chance to consider several songs that might have improved the album, while the rehearsals for 'Walls And Bridges' reveal occasional emotional depths that were later hidden by production gloss.

HERE WE GO AGAIN

The only song known to bear the writing credit Lennon/Spector, this was an outtake from the late 1973 sessions that were later salvaged for 'Rock 'n' Roll'. As this was not a rock 'n' roll classic, it failed to appear on the album and was not considered as a strong enough candidate for 'Walls And Bridges'. In many ways, it fits the mood of the latter record. Lennon begins the song in reflective mode, abruptly changing tone midway through as he becomes more anguished. There is a sense of disillusionment and defeat that permeates the song ("Everybody's an also-ran"), as Lennon testifies to an enveloping feeling of directionlessness in the midst of the 'lost weekend'. Spector adds a suitably grandiose production, using an array of instruments, most notably piano, slide guitar and orchestration.

ROCK 'N' ROLL PEOPLE

Originally cut during the sessions for 'Mind Games' back in 1973, this was an easy-going romp, which might easily have served as a warm-up for the 'Rock 'n' Roll' sessions. Lennon's voice is in fine form throughout this derivative, catch-all rock 'n' roll tribute.

ANGEL BABY

"This here is one of my favourite songs," Lennon states, while introducing this number. It's ironic then that he failed to include the track on 'Rock 'n' Roll', the more so when you consider that Morris Levy slipped it on to his unofficial release 'Roots'. Lennon's production is particularly impressive as he attempts to outdo Phil Spector as the master of the consul. The vocal is also impressive and John expertly accents the teenage angst at the core of the composition. Overall, it's far better than many of the songs that did appear on 'Rock 'n' Roll' and is an excellent addition to this album.

SINCE MY BABY LEFT ME

Better known under the title 'My Baby Left Me', this is notable for being among the most memorable songs recorded and released by Elvis Presley for Sun Records. Elvis' rockabilly version of the Arthur Crudup song featured Scooty Moore on guitar and Bill Black on bass, and Sun boss Sam Phillips was at the controls.

Lennon's version was taken from the original Phil Spector sessions in late 1973. The song is taken at a much slower tempo than expected, with a gaggle of backing singers providing an overt party atmosphere.

TO KNOW HER IS TO LOVE HER

It was most appropriate that Lennon should cover the song that gave Phil Spector his first experience of pop stardom as a member of the chart-topping Teddy Bears in 1958. Lennon had already namechecked the song on the front sleeve of 'Sometime In New York City', where there is a photo of Phil Spector encased in an apple with the motto "To Know Him Is To Love Him" written underneath. The phrase 'To Know Him Was To Love Him' was originally inscribed on the gravestone of Spector's father, before Phil altered the tense and wrote a song that became a million seller. On the record he was joined by Marshall Lieb and Annette Kleinbard, and it was the latter's distinctive voice that proved particularly memorable. Covers by male artistes obviously prompted a change of gender. Peter And Gordon altered the title to the unspecific 'To Know You Is To Love You', while Lennon preferred 'To Know Her Is To Love Her'. His version, complete with an affected and occasionally histrionic conclusion, would have been a welcome addition to 'Rock 'n' Roll'.

STEEL AND GLASS

Openly quietly, with a gentle, strumming acoustic guitar, this could almost be a reflective, introspective ballad rather than one of Lennon's more vicious put-downs. It serves as a pleasing companion piece to the more produced version on 'Walls And Bridges', with Jesse Ed Davis' solo enhancing the subdued mood. In the final verse, Lennon unexpectedly resorts to infantile insults, sneering: "There you stand with your toilet sand/And your Mickey Duck and your Donald Fuck". These words were subsequently deleted from the final version on 'Walls And Bridges', in which Lennon contented himself with a snipe at his adversary's animal instincts and backyard odour: "You leave your smell like an alley cat". In many respects, this track sounds even more menacing and direct than the previously released version.

SCARED

This is another stripped-down acoustic rehearsal, minus the Little Big Horns. Again, the sense of melancholy underlying the composition is more prevalent, with Lennon's voice painfully cracking up halfway through the song. At times, it's like hearing 'Walls And Bridges' reprogrammed in the naked manner of 'John Lennon/Plastic Ono Band'.

OLD DIRT ROAD

The strong country influence on this Lennon/Nilsson composition is even more prevalent here, with Jesse Ed Davis' guitar heard in isolation. There is also a more discernible borrowing from chain gang songs in the refrain "cool, clear water". It makes you realise how incongruous this track actually sounded amid the self-analytical material on 'Walls And Bridges'.

NOBODY LOVES YOU WHEN YOU'RE DOWN AND OUT

Although it sounds slight in relation to the full-blown version on 'Walls And Bridges', this is another interesting addendum to the Lennon catalogue. While the song seems firmly directed towards Lennon's estranged wife, the sentiments could equally apply to his demanding audience ("All I can tell you is it's all showbiz") and backstabbing music critics ("I'll scratch your back, if you knife mine"). Lennon's vocal sounds like a blunted razor at times, especially when he launches into the

"Well I get up in the morning" lament, at which the song peaks.

BLESS YOU

Lennon again has trouble staying in tune during this rehearsal as he reflects on his soured relationship with Yoko. It's a tentative and often emotional reading, but Lennon's voice cracks up rather too much for comfortable listening.

IMAGINE
John Lennon

MUSIC FROM THE MOTION PICTURE

IMAGINE: JOHN LENNON

RELEASED: OCTOBER 1988

[ORIGINAL UK ISSUE: PARLOPHONE PCSP 722]

The film soundtrack of the celebrated documentary on Lennon's life pooled together nine Beatles songs, the single version of 'Give Peace A Chance', selections from 'John Lennon/Plastic Ono Band', 'Imagine', 'Rock 'n' Roll' and 'Double Fantasy', plus the live version of 'Mother' from 'Live In New York City'. There were also two tracks, previously unavailable, as follows:

REAL LOVE

Unlike 'Free As A Bird' which was later released exclusively under the name Beatles, 'Real Love' exists as both a solo and a group recording. The song began life in 1977 under the title 'Real Life' and part of the original melody and some of the words were incorporated into 'Watching The Wheels' and 'I'm Stepping Out'. From the remaining skeleton, Lennon worked on 'Real Love', cutting seven demos of the song in late 1979. This, the sixth take, is very much a work in progress, featuring a strumming acoustic guitar and plaintive vocal. Lyrically, Lennon harks back to 'Isolation' with the line "I don't expect you to understand", which seems quite appropriate given the song's air of emotional desolation. Yoko Ono subsequently passed this song over to the remaining Beatles and it was later issued as a single and lead track of their second anthology album. The song was probably too slight to warrant the hype and lacked the sparkle and poignancy that was present in The Beatles' excellent exhumation of 'Free As A Bird'. Yet, listening to 'Real Love' as it was first presented on this album, an unheralded demo distinct from The Beatles' catalogue, its charm and potential can be better appreciated. Remarkably, this version is also of superior sound quality to the take released under The Beatles' name.

IMAGINE (REHEARSAL)

The second unreleased item on the sound-track is this two-minute rehearsal of 'Imagine', which features a croaky-voiced Lennon preparing the song for the impending studio take. Towards the end of his rendition, he slips into a country 'n' western style vocal, which is quite amusing.

Full track listing: 'Real Love'; 'Twist And Shout'; 'Help!'; 'In My Life''; 'Strawberry Fields Forever'; 'A Day In The Life'; 'Revolution'; 'The Ballad Of John & Yoko'; 'Julia'; 'Don't Let Me Down'; 'Give Peace A Chance'; 'How?'; 'Imagine (Rehearsal)'; 'God'; 'Mother'; 'Stand By Me'; 'Jealous Guy'; 'Woman'; 'Beautiful Boy'; '(Just Like) Starting Over'; 'Imagine'.

LENNON

RELEASED: OCTOBER 1990

[ORIGINAL UK ISSUE: PARLOPHONE CDS 79 5220 2]

In the continued absence of Lennon's full catalogue on CD, this boxed set offered a comprehensive introduction to the man's work. There had previously been a special issue, limited edition John Lennon boxed set issued in June 1981, but that merely collected the albums from 'Live Peace In Toronto 1969' through to 'Shaved Fish' in a gift package. This 1990 4-CD set was something much more, a genuine compilation spanning Lennon's solo work since the demise of The Beatles. Compiler Mark Lewisohn ensured that it was a decent package, with an excellent track selection, in strict chronological order. Basically, it's John Lennon denuded of Yoko Ono, whose own songs are systematically removed, although some would later appear on her own box set, 'Ono'. Apart from a couple of questionable omissions from

'Sometime In New York City', Lewisohn carefully trawls through Lennon's complete solo work to produce a representative collection. Full marks for including the groundbreaking 'John Lennon/Plastic Ono Band' in its entirety.

The only tracks on this boxed set not previously discussed are the three songs recorded live with Elton John at the Madison Square Garden on 28 November 1974.

WHATEVER GETS YOU THRU THE NIGHT (LIVE)

Lennon takes the stage and, during the tuning, the group play the opening chords of 'I Feel Fine', after which John and Elton duet on their surprise number 1 hit. It's a tentative but pleasant version with a distinct "you had to be there" feel.

LUCY IN THE SKY WITH DIAMONDS

"I wanna hear you raise the roof up to the ceiling," Elton John enthuses. "This is one of the best songs ever written." He then takes lead vocal on a reggae style version of this Lennon/McCartney classic, with John joining in the chorus.

I SAW HER STANDING THERE

Lennon concludes proceedings, by announcing: "I'd like to thank Elton and the boys for having me tonight. We're trying to think of a number to finish off with so's I can get off here and be sick. And we thought we'd do a number of an old, estranged fiancé of mine called Paul. This is one I never sang – it's an old Beatle number and we just about know it."

A rousing finale follows with this carefree version, which remains the most impressive of Lennon's three cameo appearances with Elton John.

Full track listing: 'Give Peace A Chance'; 'Blue Suede Shoes'; 'Money (That's What I Want)'; 'Dizzy Miss Lizzy'; 'Yer Blues'; 'Cold Turkey'; 'Instant Karma!'; 'Mother'; 'Hold On'; 'I Found Out'; 'Working Class Hero'; 'Isolation'; 'Remember'; 'Love'; 'Well Well Well'; 'Look At Me'; 'God'; 'My Mummy's Dead'; 'Power To The People'; 'Well (Baby Please Don't Go)'; 'Imagine'; 'Crippled Inside'; 'Jealous Guy'; 'It's So Hard'; 'Gimme Some Truth'; 'Oh My Love'; 'How Do You Sleep?'; 'Oh Yoko!'; 'Happy Xmas (War Is Over)'; 'Woman Is The Nigger Of The World'; 'New York City'; 'John Sinclair'; 'Come Together'; 'Hound Dog'; 'Mind Games'; 'Aisumasen (I'm Sorry)'; 'One Day (At A Time)';

'Intuition'; 'Out Of The Blue'; 'Whatever Gets You Thru The Night'; 'Going Down On Love'; 'Old Dirt Road'; 'Bless You'; 'Scared'; '# 9 Dream'; 'Surprise Surprise (Sweet Bird Of Paradox)'; 'Steel And Glass'; 'Nobody Loves You (When You're Down And Out)'; 'Stand By Me'; 'Ain't That A Shame'; 'Do You Want To Dance'; 'Sweet Little Sixteen'; 'Slippin' And Slidin''; 'Angel Baby'; 'Just Because'; 'Whatever Gets You Thru The Night (Live Version)'; 'Lucy In The Sky With Diamonds'; 'I Saw Her Standing There'; '(Just Like) Starting Over'; 'Cleanup Time'; 'I'm Losing You'; 'Beautiful Boy (Darling Boy)'; 'Watching The Wheels'; 'Woman'; 'Dear Yoko'; 'I'm Stepping Out'; 'I Don't Wanna Face It'; 'Nobody Told Me'; 'Borrowed Time'; '(Forgive Me) My Little Flower Princess'; 'Every Man Has A Woman Who Loves Him'; 'Grow Old With Me'.

SINGLES

The following singles are UK issues, unless otherwise stated. American releases offering different track selections are featured in chronological order. Chart placings are included, courtesy of *Music Week* (UK) and *Billboard* (US).

'Give Peace A Chance'/ 'Remember Love'

Apple 13. Released July 1969. Credited to The Plastic Ono Band, this single reached number 2 in the UK charts and number 14 in the US. The B-side, a quietly sung Yoko Ono ballad, was also first recorded in Room 1742 of Hotel La Reine Elizabeth, Montreal, with John on acoustic guitar.

'Cold Turkey'/'Don't Worry Kyoko (Mummy's Only Looking For Her Hand In The Snow)'

Apple 1001. Released October 1969. Credited to The Plastic Ono Band, this single reached number 14 in the UK charts and number 30 in the US. The B-side was arguably Yoko Ono's greatest recorded moment, with Lennon, Clapton, Voormann and Starr providing a riveting backing.

'Instant Karma!'/'Who Has Seen The Wind'

Apple 1003. Released February 1970. Credited to Lennon/Ono with The Plastic Ono Band, this reached number 5 in the UK charts and number 3 in the US. The B-side, sung like a nursery rhyme in Yoko's slight voice, was augmented by tambourine and woodwind.

'Mother'/'Why'

Apple 1827. US Release December 1970. Credited to Lennon/Ono with The Plastic Ono Band, this single reached number 43 in the US. The B-side featured Yoko Ono at her most intense, screaming against a solid rock backing.

'Power To The People'/'Open Your Box'

Apple R 5892. Released March 1971. Co-credited to The Plastic Ono Band, this reached number 7 in the UK charts. The B-side featured Yoko warbling wildly, aided

by some of John's experimental guitar work.

'Power To The People'/'Touch Me'

Apple 1830. US Release March 1971. Co-credited to The Plastic Ono Band, this reached number 11 in the US charts. The B-side featured another highly wrought performance by Yoko, reinforced by the instrumental contributions of Lennon, Voormann and Starr.

'Imagine'/'It's So Hard'

Apple 1840. US Release October 1971. This double selection from the album 'Imagine' reached number 3 in the US charts.

'Happy Xmas (War Is Over)'/ 'Listen The Snow Is Falling'

Apple R 5970. Released November 1972. Credited to John & Yoko/The Plastic Ono Band With The Harlem Community Choir, this single was first released in the US, where it failed to chart, in December 1971. Due to a publishing dispute it was postponed in the UK for almost a year. It reached number 4 in the UK charts in 1972 and number 2 in 1980. The B-side featured Yoko Ono's hymn to Christmas, complete with references to the Empire State Building and Trafalgar Square. Lennon provided the reverb guitar.

'Woman Is The Nigger Of The World'/'Sisters O Sisters'

Apple 1848. US Release April 1972. Regrettably, this single failed to reach the US Top 40, peaking at a lowly number 57. It was unissued in the UK due to the publishing dispute concerning Yoko Ono's writing collaboration.

'Mind Games'/'Meat City'

Apple R 5994. Released November 1973. This reached number 26 in the UK charts and number 18 in the US.

'Whatever Gets You Thru The Night'/ 'Beef Jerky'

Apple R 5998. Released October 1974. This reached number 26 in the UK charts and number 1 in the US.

'# 9 Dream'/'What You Got'

Apple R 6003. Released January 1975. This reached number 23 in the UK charts and number 9 in the US.

'Stand By Me'/'Move Over Ms L'

Apple R 6005. Released April 1975. This reached number 30 in the UK charts and number 20 in the US. The irreverent B-side was a rare example of a John Lennon track unavailable on album, although it was subsequently included on the CD version of 'The John Lennon Collection'.

'Imagine'/'Working Class Hero'

Apple 6009. Released October 1975. This reached number 6 in the UK charts after its belated release in 1975, and number 1 in 1980.

'(Just Like) Starting Over'/ 'Kiss Kiss Kiss'

Geffen K 79186. Released October 1980. This reached number 1 in both the UK and US charts.

'Woman'/'Beautiful Boys'

Geffen K 79185. Released January 1981. This reached number 1 in the UK charts and number 2 in the US.

'Watching The Wheels'/'I'm Your Angel'

Geffen K79207. Released March 1981. This reached number 30 in the UK charts and number 10 in the US.

'Love'/'Give Me Some Truth'

Parlophone R 6059. Released November 1982.

'Nobody Told Me'/'O Sanity'

Polydor POSP 700. Released January 1984. This reached number 6 in the UK charts and number 5 in the US.

'Borrowed Time'/'Your Hands'

Polydor POSP 701. Released March 1984. This reached number 32 in the UK charts.

'Borrowed Time'/'Your Hands'/ 'Never Say Goodbye'

Polydor POSPX 701. Released March 1984.

'Give Peace A Chance'/'Cold Turkey'

EMI G45 2. Released March 1984.

'I'm Stepping Out'/'Sleepless Night'

Polydor POSP 702. Released July 1984. This single reached number 55 in the US charts.

'I'm Stepping Out'/ 'Sleepless Night'/'Loneliness'

Polydor POSPX 702. Released July 1984.

'Every Man Has A Woman Who Loves Him'/'It's Alright'

Polydor POSP 712. Released November 1984.

'Jealous Guy'/'Going Down On Love'

Parlophone R 6117. Released November 1985. This single reached number 65 in the UK charts.

'Jealous Guy'/'Going Down On Love'/'Oh Yoko!'

Parlophone 12R 6117. Released November 1985.

'Jealous Guy'/'Give Peace A Chance'

Capitol B 442230. Released September 1988. This single reached a lowly number 80 in the US charts.

'Imagine'/'Jealous Guy'

Parlophone R 6199. Released December 1988.This single reached number 45 in the UK.

'Imagine'/'Jealous Guy'/'Happy Xmas (War Is Over)'

Parlophone 6199. Released December 1988.

'Imagine'/'Jealous Guy'/'Happy Xmas (War Is Over)'/'Give Peace A Chance'

Parlophone CDR 6119. Released December 1988.

GUEST APPEARANCES

During his Beatles' years, Lennon contributed songs to several acts in the Brian Epstein stable, including Billy J. Kramer And The Dakotas, The Fourmost and Silkie. However, apart from a backing vocal on The Rolling Stones' 'We Love You', his guest appearances during the Sixties appear to have been minimal. Once he met Yoko Ono and left The Beatles though, he was a lot freer to tackle different projects. This section documents his extra-curricular songwriting, production credits and guest appearances on other artistes' records.

YOKO ONO ALBUM RELEASES

'Yoko Ono/Plastic Ono Band'

Released: December 1970; Apple SAP-COR 17. Lennon produced and contributed guitar to this album.

'Fly'

Released: December 1971; Apple

SAPTU 101/2. Lennon co-produced and contributed guitar to this album.

'Approximately Infinite Universe'
Released: February 1973; Apple SAPDO 1001. Lennon co-produced and appeared on part of this album, most noticeably 'Move On Fast'. The album is dedicated to John: "my best friend of the second sex".

'Feeling The Space'
Released: November 1973; Apple SAP-COR 26. Lennon appeared on three tracks: 'She Hits Back', 'Woman Power' and 'Men Men Men'.

'Season Of Glass'
Released: June 1981; Geffen K 99164. This album included a free copy of the single 'Walking On Thin Ice'/'It Happened' [Geffen K 79202; originally released February 1981], both sides of which were co-produced by Lennon. Yoko: "'Walking On Thin Ice' was what we were remixing that night [8 December 1980]. The past weekend we had listened to the song all day and all night. It was as if we were both haunted by the song. I remember I woke up in the morning and found John watching the sunrise and still listening to the song. He said I had to put it out right away as a single".

'Every Man Has A Woman'
Released: September 1984; Polydor POLH 13. This various artistes' compilation of Ono material, included a previously unissued performance of 'Every Man Has A Woman Who Loves Him', retitled 'Every Man Has A Woman', featuring John Lennon on vocals.

'Ono'
Released March 1992; Rykodisc RCD 10224/9. This retrospective 6-CD boxed set featured many tracks that Yoko had recorded or co-produced with Lennon from 'Life With The Lions' onwards.

OTHER LENNON RELATED RELEASES

Aspen

Published: March 1969 The spring/summer edition of the arts magazine *Aspen* included a flexi-disc featuring tracks from the soon-to-be-released 'Unfinished Music No 2: Life With The Lions'. As well as 'No Bed For Beatle John' and 'Radio Play', the magazine premièred a recording that failed to make the final album listing: 'Song For John'. This was effectively an ad-libbed medley of three of Yoko's songs: 'Let's Go On Flying', 'Snow Is Falling All The Time' and 'Don't Worry Kyoko (Mummy's Only Looking For Her Hand In The Snow)'.

'God Save Us'/ 'Do The Oz'

Bill Elliot And The Elastic Oz Band. Released: July 1971; Apple 36. Lennon produced and composed both sides of this single and sang on the B-side. It was issued as part of a fund-raising appeal for the infamous *OZ* obscenity trial. Full page advertisements, funded by the Lennons, appeared in the underground press, proclaiming: "Every country has a screw in its side, in England, it's *OZ*. *OZ* is on trial for its life. John and Yoko have written and helped produce this record – the proceeds of which are going to *OZ* to help pay their legal fees. The entire British underground is in trouble, it needs our help. Please listen – 'God Save *Oz*'."

The record failed to sell enough copies to register a chart entry.

'The Pope Smokes Dope'

David Peel And The Lower East Side. Released (US): April 1972; Apple 1839. Lennon produced and guested on this album, which did not receive a UK release.

'Elephant's Memory'

Released: November 1972; Apple SAP-COR 22. Lennon produced this album from his backing group and also appeared on several tracks.

'Ringo'

Ringo Starr. Released: November 1973; Apple PCTC 252. Lennon wrote, played and sang on the track 'I'm The Greatest'.

'Pussy Cats'

Nilsson. Released: August 1974; RCA APL 1-0570. Lennon produced this album and wrote the track 'Mucho Mungo', which Nilsson placed in a medley with his own 'Mt Elba'.

'Goodnight Vienna'

Ringo Starr. Released: November 1974; Apple PCS 7168. Lennon co-wrote and appeared on the title track, and also played on 'Only You' and 'All By Myself'.

'Lucy In The Sky With Diamonds'/ 'One Day At A Time'

Elton John. Released: November 1974; DJM DJS 340. Lennon co-wrote the A-side, wrote the B-side and guested on both sides of this single.

'Save The Last Dance For Me'/ 'All My Life'

Nilsson. Released: January 1975; RCA 2504. Lennon produced both sides of this single.

'Philadelphia Freedom'/ 'I Saw Her Standing There'

Elton John. Released: February 1975; DJM DJS 354. Lennon appeared on the B-side of this single, which was credited to the Elton John Band featuring John Lennon & The Muscle Shoals Horns. The track re-appeared on an Elton John single in 1981 and also featured on the posthumous compilation album 'Lennon'.

'Young Americans'

David Bowie. Released: March 1975; RCA RS 1006. Lennon co-wrote the tracks 'Across The Universe' and 'Fame' and sang and played on both versions on this album. 'Fame' was issued as a single by Bowie and reached number 1 in the US charts.

'Ringo's Rotogravure'

Ringo Starr. Released: September 1976; Polydor 2382 040. Lennon wrote and played on the song 'Cookin'', a composition he never released under his own name.

'I Saw Her Standing There'/ 'Whatever Gets You Thru The Night'/ 'Lucy In The Sky With Diamonds'

Elton John Band Featuring John Lennon & The Muscle Shoals Horns. Released: March 1981. DJM DJS 10965. This single featured the three songs that Lennon performed with Elton John at the Madison Square Garden on 28 November 1974. All three were subsequently included on the 4-CD compilation boxed set 'Lennon'.

'Playground Psychotics'

Frank Zappa/The Mothers. Released October 1992; Rykodisc RCD 10557/58. As Frank Zappa's liner notes explain: "Some of you might have heard another version of this material on the John & Yoko album, 'Sometime In New York City'. When they sat in with us that night, we were in the process of recording the 'Live At the Fillmore East, June 1971' album, and all of this insanity was captured on tape. After the show, John and I agreed we would each put out our own version of the performance, and I gave him a copy of the 16-track master tape. Here is our version – a substantially different mix from what they released."

Zappa's mix sounds a lot clearer than the Lennons' version. He retitles part of the jam, with a new track listing that reads: 'Well', 'Say Please', 'Aaawk', Scum Bag' and 'A Small Eternity With Yoko Ono'. He also edits both the encore screams and closing music played over the PA.

INDEX